Wild truth

Bible Lessons 2

12 more wild studies for junior highers, based on wild Bible characters

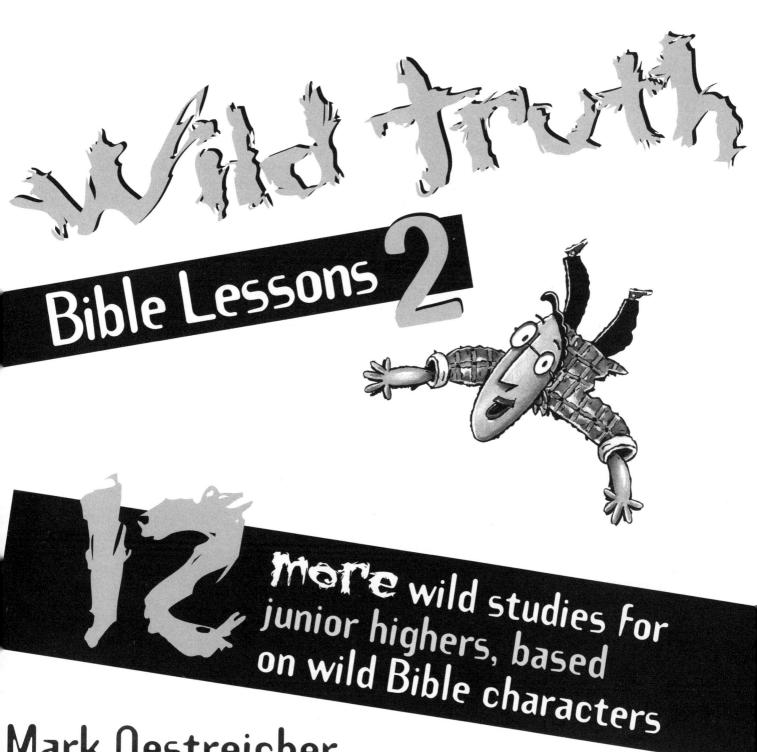

Wild truth

Bible Lessons 2

12 more wild studies for junior highers, based on wild Bible characters

Mark Oestreicher

Youth Specialties

ZONDERVAN

A DIVISION OF HARPERCOLLINS*PUBLISHERS*

*Wild Truth Bible Lessons 2: 12 **more** wild studies for junior highers, based on wild Bible characters*

Copyright ©1998 by Youth Specialties

Youth Specialties Books, 300 S. Pierce St., El Cajon, CA 92020, are published by Zondervan, 5300 Patterson Ave. S.E., Grand Rapids, MI 49530.

Library of Congress Cataloging-in-Publication Data

Oestreicher, Mark.
    Wild truth Bible lessons 2 : 12 more wild studies for junior highers, based on wild Bible characters / Mark Oestreicher.
        p.   cm.
    ISBN 0-310-22024-6 (alk. paper)
    1. Christian education of teenagers. 2. Christian education of children. 3. Bible—Biography—Study and teaching. 4. Junior high school students—Religious life. I. Title.
    BV1561.O38 1998
    268'.433—dc21   97-45509
                                                                CIP

Unless otherwise indicated, all Scripture quotations are taken from the *Holy Bible: New International Version* (North American Edition). Copyright ©1973, 1978, 1984 by International Bible Society. Used by permission of Zondervan Publishing House.

Edited by Vicki Newby
Cover and interior design by Patton Brothers Design

Printed in the United States of America

07 08 09 / ML / 12 11 10 9

To Gordon Kirk, senior pastor of Lake Avenue Church. Thanks for your commitment to the Word of God, your leadership, and your friendship. And thanks for taking a chance on a junior high guy like me.

CONTENTS

INTRO...9

1. Shad, Shaq, & Abe, the Firemen *Shadrach, Meshach, & Abednego (standing up for what you believe)*...11

2. Hanny, the Wannabe Nanny *Hannah (prayer)*...19

3. Joe's Bros, the Sibling Sellers *Joseph's brothers (responding when someone offends you)*...25

4. Hard-Knocks Pablo *The apostle Paul (on persecution and hardships)*...33

5. Andy & Sophie, the King and Queen of Lies *Ananias & Sapphira (lying)*...41

6. Richie Rich, the Material Boy *The rich young ruler (materialism)*...47

7. Roof Club, the Extra-Mile Friends *The stretcher bearers who lowered their friend through a roof to Jesus (meeting your friends' needs)*...55

8. Hammerhead, the Nap-Time Monitor *Jael (doing difficult things for God)*...61

9. Bad Luck Boils *Job (when life is unfair)*...67

10. Sam, the Mighty Man *Samson (making choices based on values rather than on experience)*..75

11. Giddy, the Frightened Wimp *Gideon (how God sees us)*...83

12. Weather Man *Jesus (his power in the middle of your problems)*...89

ACKNOWLEDGMENTS

Thanks to my wonderful family—Jeannie, Liesl, and Max for graciously giving me writing time…to Todd Temple, my idea whip, "agent," and friend…to Tim McLaughlin, an editor without equal…to the junior highers and volunteer staff of Lake Avenue Church for your friendship…and to Mark and Stephanie Riddle, Jimmy Doyle, and Jordan "the intern" for the 10-foot-pole and the Kung Fu Bible Theater ideas.

EXPERIMENTS IN FAITH

Although most people don't consider the Bible a science book, it clearly is in at least one sense. For many of the best passages in Scripture tell the stories of ancient *experiments in faith*. These biblical accounts tell us what happened when believers dared the unthinkable: *to live God's truth.*

It's significant that although the people in these experiments are dead and buried, the God they encountered isn't. This same God is still alive, still at work. And his truth still matters. That means we can use these stories as *research data*—we can relive the best parts of the old experiments to see if we can duplicate the best results. When we do, we prove again that God's truth is timeless. It's as good today as it was back then.

Of course you already know that. You relive these experiments in your own life, growing in your knowledge and love of God with each new discovery. *But how do you get your junior highers to know this?*

That's what the **Wild Truth** series is all about. Each lesson takes your students on an adventure back to a Bible story, to explore an ancient experiment in faith. What did these old faith-searchers discover about God and his truth? How did they *apply* the truth? What was the *result*?

And here's the best part. After the research comes the *re-enactment*. Each **Wild Truth** lesson ends with a practical application: a challenge to re-enact the ancient experiment today. It's not enough for your students to know the truth—they must dare to live the truth. And that's when the truth gets *wild*.

Each lesson in this book is organized to take your students on such an experimental journey. Here are the four steps:

JUMP START helps you bring your students together in a fun way—and helps them set aside distractions and instead focus on the lesson's theme.

GETTING THE POINT lays out the basic point of the lesson, giving your group a clear idea of what today's experiment is all about.

FLASHBACK takes your students on a journey back to an ancient experiment, to discover what happened when the faith-searcher dared to live God's truth.

FAST FORWARD returns your group to the here and now, to re-enact the best parts of the experiment by applying the truth to their own lives today.

More Wild Truth

The 12 Bible characters studied in this book were selected from Mark Oestreicher's *Wild Truth Journal*—a devotional journal for junior highers, containing 50 short character studies and applications (and, like this book, published by Youth Specialties/10 TO 20 Press). *WTJ* has lots of cool graphics, engaging questions and quizzes, and plenty of room for writing (it's a journal, after all). Of course you don't need *WTJ* to teach from *Wild Truth Bible Lessons* 2, but many youth leaders have told us that they use the journal as a support tool to their teaching. Here's how you can use the *Wild Truth Journal* to augment the lessons in this book:

• Assign the journal's personal lesson as a setup or follow-up to your group teaching. (Kind of like homework, but a lot more fun.)

• If you find an illustration or activity in the journal that works better for your group than the material suggested in this book, replace it.

• Hand out copies of *Wild Truth Journal* at your next camp or retreat, where students can use the journal during their daily devotions—and then continue using the journals during their devotions or quiet times back home.

• When you run out of lessons in this book, write your own material using the other characters in the journal. Just use the four-step plan from this book to build on the journal content. Mark Oestreicher has already done this for 12 other characters from the journal, in *Wild Truth Bible Lessons* (but you probably already figured that out, since this book has a "2" in the title).

    You can pick up copies of *Wild Truth Journal* and *Wild Truth Bible Lessons* at your Christian bookstore or by calling Youth Specialties' order center at 800-776-8008.

Wild Times

If you're unfamiliar with the author's writing and teaching, you're in for a treat. Mark Oestreicher's love for junior highers and delight in teaching them the truth of God is revealed on every page. His sense of humor was a prerequisite to his successes with this special age, and it has clearly grown as a result of long years (and long nights) in junior high ministry. As you read his book, be assured that you are listening to a comrade who empathizes with you in your ministry and applauds the often thankless yet absolutely essential work you do.

    Together, you and the author are living and teaching God's unstoppable, earth-shattering, life-altering, Wild Truth to an unstoppable, earth-shattering, life-altering age. The likeness is no coincidence.

Todd Temple
10 TO 20 Press

Shad, Shaq, & Abe the Firemen

Shadrach, Meshach, & Abednego, on standing up for what you believe

Bible passage: Daniel 3:1-30

SHAD, SHAQ & ABE

GOALS

Students will—

- *Identify some of their convictions and beliefs.*
- *Understand that if they live for God, they will, at some time, be called on to stand up for those convictions in the face of opposition.*
- *Decide which convictions and beliefs they're willing to stand by.*

JUMP START

I Believe It!

Set up chairs in rows—with plenty of space between them—enough for all the kids, and have them take a seat. Then explain to your group that you're going to force them to declare some of their beliefs. Tell them these beliefs could be about a whole variety of subjects: religion, politics, morality, whatever. You'll say a number and a direction, like 3 to the right, and then state a belief. If they agree with that belief, they should shout, "I believe it!" and move as many seats as you specified. You may have played a game similar to this, but without the teaching value—this will get kids to identify values and beliefs while having fun.

You'll need—
- *no materials*

Explain that the rows, sideways and forward and back, are continuous. So if Rick only has one seat on his left side and has to move three to the left, he should go to the other end of the row to move in two seats. If someone is already in the seat, he sits on the waiting lap (your kids will groan at this point). In fact there may already be two or three or more people—just stack up and hope you can move soon!

Now read this list and watch the madness ensue! You'll have to remind kids of the rules here and there. And you may have to prod a kid who isn't moving at all. When you state a belief you're sure the student holds, question her about it specifically.

- **Move 2 to the right if you believe in yourself.**
- **Move 3 to the left if you believe Jesus is God's Son.**
- **Move 1 to the right if you believe in the death penalty.**
- **Move 5 back if you believe abortion is okay in some situations.**
- **Move 4 to the left if you believe extraterrestrial life exists.**
- **Move 2 forward if you believe love is an action.**
- **Move 4 to the right if you believe in love at first sight.**
- **Move 1 to the right if you believe the butler did it.**
- **Move 2 to the left if you believe racial tension is getting worse.**
- **Move 3 back if you believe Christ will return during your lifetime.**
- **Move 3 to the right if you believe you will be famous someday.**
- **Move 1 to the left if you believe in a hell with literal flames.**
- **Move 2 to the right if you believe CDs cost too much.**
- **Move 5 forward if you believe guys are smarter than girls.**

When these three young Hebrew captives were brought back to Babylon from the recent sack of Jerusalem, their potential was quickly recognized. They were fast-tracked through a subsidized education in Babylonian arts and sciences into government jobs as royal advisors. Then came the statue affair—jealousy and bureaucratic backstabbing that resulted in the conviction of a capital crime. Expecting no miracle but only certain death, the three nonetheless let their king know—tactfully yet pointedly—that being burned alive was no big deal compared to keeping faith with their God.

- Move 4 to the right if you believe girls are smarter than guys.
- Move 2 to the left if you believe pizza is good food.
- Move 1 to the left if you believe animals will go to heaven.
- Move 3 back if you believe home schooling is a good idea.
- Move 6 to the right if you believe the government knows all about you.
- Move 4 forward if you believe war is necessary sometimes.
- Move 5 to the right if you believe money will solve all your problems.
- Move 2 to the left if you believe you look like one of your parents.
- Move 1 to the right if you believe gym class is cruel and unusual punishment.
- Go back to where you started if you believe you'd like to return to your original seat.

Once students are settled back in their seats, ask:

- What are some other things you believe?
- Name one thing you think you believe but you're not completely sure about.
- How about one thing that you believe so strongly, nothing could make you change your mind about it?

GETTING THE POINT
You Are What You Believe

Distribute copies of **You Are What You Believe** (page 15) and a pencil or pen to each of your students. Ask them to write five beliefs they hold about Christianity, the Bible, or God. Some of your students may need a little help with this (some may need a *lot* of help with this!). Circulate among them, and offer suggestions—ideas they can rewrite as beliefs:

You'll need—
- *copies of You Are What You Believe (page 15)*
- *pens or pencils*

- I believe Jesus is God's Son.
- I believe Jesus died on the cross and rose from the dead.
- I believe the Bible is God's truth and is accurate.
- I believe God knows everything about me and loves me.
- I believe Jesus will return again.
- I believe a relationship with God, through Jesus, is the only way to heaven.
- I believe that I've been justified by the vicarious atonement of Jesus Christ, God incarnate, as the propitiation for our sins, and that big words impress people.

After each kid has written a set of beliefs (hopefully, since they've only written five, these will be five of their strongest beliefs), have several share one or two with the whole group. Then ask them to add a needle to the strength-of-conviction meters next to each belief to show how strongly they hold their beliefs.

Finally, have your students pick an answer from the list (or they can write in their own) that reflects their feelings about this question: At what point would I give up this belief? The idea is to test the strength of their convictions. In other words, are they willing to die or to be teased or to lose a finger for the belief?

After they've completed this last step, ask your students to reflect on the strength of their convictions about their personal beliefs. Generally, are they committed to their beliefs? Or are they pretty wishy-washy about them? Have a few share out loud.

FLASHBACK

Shad, Shaq, & Abe—the Firemen

Say: We're going to look at a story many of you have heard before. It's a story about a group of friends who were really committed to their beliefs—so committed they were willing to die for them. I need some volunteers to help me, people who are willing to act a little bit.

You'll need—
• one copy of *Shad, Shaq, & Abe—the Firemen* (page 16)
• Bibles

Recruit the following roles:

SHAD	THE TATTLETALES (TWO KIDS)
SHAQ	THE YOUNG WOMEN OF THE
ABE	KINGDOM (TWO GIRLS)
THE KING	THE MUSICIANS
AN ANGEL	(THREE KIDS TO PLAY
THE FIRE STOKER	IN AN AIR BAND)
THE BIG OL' IDOL	

If you have a small group, and this is too many roles, have some play more than one part You could even play a role if you feel thespianically inclined (yeah, I know *thespianically* isn't a word—just work with me, okay?).

Read the narration yourself, and have the actors play their parts with flourish. Encourage them to ham it up (of course, Shad, Shaq, and Abe, being good Jewish boys, would never have had anything to do with ham). When you read a line of dialogue, the actor should repeat it in character. Make sure you pause for the actors to say their lines and act out their parts.

After the melodrama is finished, give a big ol' round of applause to the actors. Then read your group the story in Daniel 3:1-30, or ask the students to read it with you in their Bibles.

After you read the passage, ask these questions:

• **Why was the king ticked at Shadrach, Meschach, and Abednego?** [They wouldn't bow down to his idol.]

• **Why do you think the king cared that they wouldn't worship his idol?** [His ego was on the line—everyone else had bowed down; so it would look like he was powerless over these guys if they set their own standards.]

• **Do you think Shadrach, Meschach, and Abednego were making a big deal out of nothing? Would it have mattered at all if they had bowed down physically but not *really worshipped* the idol? Why or why not?** [It mattered because these three guys were convinced that God wanted them to worship only him—without even *looking* like they were worshipping someone or something else.]

• **Which of these is the best summary of Shadrach, Meschach, and Abednego's response to the king's demands in verses 16-18?**

   1. "King, we know, beyond a shadow of a doubt, that if you toss us into the fire, our God will protect us and we won't burn."

   2. King, we know our God can save us, and we hope he will. But even if he chooses not to save us, we won't bow down to your idol." [This is the one.]

   3. King, you are one amazingly large windbag—full of steaming hot air! We will never bow down to your stupid idol, you self-serving pompous pig!"

• **What, if anything, strikes you as really cool about their response?** [The guys hoped for rescue, knowing God was capable. But they seemed to be fully content to allow God to make the decision whether or not he would save them. They were willing to be toast!]

Wrap up this section by saying something like this: God never promised us that we would live a breezy, happy, shiny life if we follow him. In fact, he promises us the opposite. If you live for God, there will come a time when you need to stand up for your convictions—and the result may not be pretty. Remember that God promises to be with you all the time. Nothing, absolutely nothing—not even big ol' flames in a fiery furnace or a mean stuck-up king—can separate you from God's love.

Yo! King Nebbie! It's Me Calling!

Pass out copies of **Yo! King Nebbie! It's Me Calling!** (page 18) to each student. They should already have pens or pencils. And by now, if your students are within 25 degrees of normal for junior highers, they will have used their pens or pencils in one or more of the following helpful non-Martha Stewart-approved ways:

• As cute little swords for reenactments of Old Testament battles (or just bugging their neighbors by poking them)

• As extremely accurate hole creators, turning **You Are What You Believe** into an effective vegetable strainer or window screen

• As medieval tools of destruction, defacing every piece of church property in sight

• Or as deconstruction case studies, splintering the wood of the pencil or the parts of the pen into multiple smaller units

So...ask them to pull out these wonderful marking devices and look at **Yo! King Nebbie! It's Me Calling!**, which you have just handed them. Then ask your junior highers to think back to the beliefs they wrote down on **You Are What You Believe.**

Say: Is there anything that you're wimping out on? Are there any convictions you hold that people would be surprised to find out about? Choose one conviction you need to be a little stronger—or a lot stronger—about, and write it in the first space on *Yo! King Nebbie! It's Me Calling!*

After a couple minutes, ask your kids to think of one person, one King Nebbie, they need to make this conviction more clear to. They should write that person's name in the second space.

Finally, challenge them to think how they might take a stand on this issue. Ask them to write a simple plan of action in the third space. After all this writing is complete, have a few volunteers share their whole plans. It would be best if you share a personal response, too.

Be sure to close in prayer, asking God to give everyone courage to stand up for truth, to defend their beliefs and convictions, and to rely on God's strength in times of testing.

YOU ARE WHAT YOU BELIEVE

Five-o-My Beliefs

In this coulmn, write five beliefs you hold about God, Christianity, or the Bible. C'mon, you can come up with five! Finish this before going on.

Strength

Draw a needle on each of the strength-of-conviction meters to reflect how strongly you hold to each particular statement:

- *1 means*—Puhleeeeze, I don't even know why I wrote this—I don't really even believe it!

- *10 means*—I believe this so strongly, you could pull out my nose hairs one at a time, and it still wouldn't change my belief! Finish this before going on.

Breaking Point

What would it take to get you to give up this belief? Pick from the list below, or think up your own idea. Write your choice for each belief in this column.

1.

2.

3.

4.

5.

BREAKING POINT OPTIONS

- Being covered with honey and having 1,000 bees sit on me
- Someone breaking one of my fingers
- Someone pulling out all my teeth
- Having my eyes gouged out

- Teasing from people I don't know
- Teasing from my good friends
- Teasing from my family
- Mean ridicule from my best friends and family
- Everyone I know turning their backs on me

- Being put in jail overnight
- Being put in jail for a weekend
- Being put in prison for ten years
- Someone killing all my family
- No breaking point—even death wouldn't change my mind

SHAD, SHAQ, & ABE—THE FIREMEN

a melodrama for way too many people

Characters
- Shad
- Shaq
- Abe
- The king
- An angel
- The fire stoker

- The musicians (three kids to play in an air band)
- The big ol' idol
- The tattletales (two kids)
- The young women of the kingdom (two girls)

After a long and nasty battle, a new king came into power. He was pretty happy with himself and often strutted around his castle saying things like, "I'm really happy with myself" and "I couldn't be much happier with myself." But the king actually was kinda smart, and he knew that in order to win over the people of the land he had invaded, he would do good to brainwash some of their best and brightest.

So the king called in some of his advisors, the Tattletales, and gave them these instructions: "Look all over the land, and bring me a few good men. They must be *extremely* good looking, totally smart, great at every sport, good at speaking, and basically complete and total studs!"

The advisors searched the land and found a bunch of guys, including Shad, Shaq, and Abe—three of the biggest stud-men in the whole country. In fact, they were so gorgeous, every time they walked past the young women of the kingdom, the young women would swoon and make loud sighing noises. They were so smart, every time they would walk past the young women of the kingdom, the young women would say, "Ooh, they're soooooo smart!" And they were such total all-around studs, that every time they would walk past the young women of the kingdom, the young women would faint.

Well, the king tried to brainwash them. But all he ended up doing was giving them a good education. They prayed to God all the time, asking him to give them strength to serve the king well and live clean lives for God. This ticked off the Tattletales. In fact, they would stomp around their rooms, jumping up and down, shouting, "It's not fair, It's not fair! We're better than those guys!" They stomped some more and shouted, "We should do something about this!" So they came up with a plan.

One day the Tattletales visited the king in his throne room. They bowed down in front of him and said things like, "Oh super king—you're the greatest! You're the mostest awesomest King ever!" And stuff like that. Of course, the king liked this and asked them to say some more good stuff—which they did. Then they laid out their plan.

"King," they said, in unison, "you should make a big ol' idol, kinda representing you. Then you should get a really cool band and have them play loud music. And every time the music is played, everyone in the kingdom should bow down and worship the idol." Once again, the king thought this was a pretty good idea.

"Yeah," he said, "a big ol' idol of me!"

And then the Tattletales added, "And if anyone won't bow down to the idol— toast 'em."

"Yeah," said the king, "toast 'em." So he had the idol built.

Once the idol was done, the band started playing right in front of it. They seriously jammed! They jumped around and screamed and played their instruments at an ear-shattering volume. And everyone, including the Tattletales, bowed down and worshipped the idol. Everyone, that is, except three guys— Shad, Shaq, and Abe.

They stood a long way off and shouted, "We're not gonna bow!"

And the Tattletales ran to the king, started jumping up and down with excitement (they seemed to like jumping up and down), and singing, "Shad, Shaq, and Abe wouldn't bow. Let's toast 'em!" They sang it over and over again, making a little song out of it.

The king was ticked! So he gave an order to the fire stoker to heat up the big ol' royal furnace, and to make it seriously hot. Then the fire stoker brought Shad, Shaq, and Abe to the top edge of the furnace and tossed 'em in. The fire was so hot it totally fried the fire stoker.

But something strange happened. When the king looked in the furnace, he saw Shad, Shaq, and Abe walking around and talking to a fourth guy—an angel! In fact, the four were kinda doing a little shuffle dance, like the hokey-pokey or something. The king called for them to be pulled out of the fire. And when they came out—nothing on them was even burnt or smoky. The king passed a new law that anyone could worship God, and that anyone who said anything against God would be chopped up into little pieces! Gross! Everyone danced around and praised God—except the Tattletales, who pouted in the corner.

WILDPAGE

Yo! King Nebbie! It's Me Calling!

One belief or conviction I'm a little wimpy on:

My King Nebbie—the person I need to be more clear with about this conviction:

My plan of action:

✂ -

WILDPAGE

Yo! King Nebbie! It's Me Calling!

One belief or conviction I'm a little wimpy on:

My King Nebbie—the person I need to be more clear with about this conviction:

My plan of action:

Hanny
the Wannabe Nanny

Hannah, on prayer

Bible passage: 1 Samuel 1:2-28

GOALS

Students will—

• *Understand how prayer works.*

• *Make a list of things to pray about.*

• *Spend time praying.*

JUMP START

Speak and Listen!

Start the time by asking your students these questions:

• **What's the purpose of talking?** [To communicate information.]

• **What's the purpose of listening?** [To gather information.]

• **Which are you better at: talking or listening?**

You'll need—
• *copies of Speak and Listen! (page 22) cut into pieces*

Ask your students to pair up. Help those who don't have friends in your group to find a partner without feeling singled out or weird. (This is best accomplished by having those students stand up, pointing at them, and shouting, "Who'll pair up with this friendless geek? Okay, on second thought, maybe you shouldn't say that; just be aware of those who need help pairing up.)

After everyone's settled, tell the kids they're going to experience a little communications challenge. They're

going to have to speak clearly and listen well.

Ask: **Have you ever done one of those puzzles where you look for the hidden objects in a picture? We're going to do a verbal version of one of those.**

Pass out the strips you've copied and cut from **Speak and Listen!** (page 22). Pass them out in pairs—in other words, each pair of kids should get a Version 1 and a Version 2. Give them clear instructions that they are not, under any circumstances, to look at each other's slips of paper (which would ruin the activity).

Instruct the people with Version 1 to clearly read their paragraph aloud, so the other person has no problem hearing it. Students are not allowed to read it more than once or repeat or clarify anything. And once they've read it (this is important), they are to fold it in half and not look at it again.

After this first step is complete, the second student does the exact same thing with her paragraph: Read it clearly to the first person without repeating anything, then fold it in half and do not look at it again.

Finally, ask the two to figure out the seven differences between their two paragraphs. Seven factual items or descriptions are different in each pair of paragraphs. After a few minutes, ask if they were able to think of all seven; then allow them to look at their paragraphs again and find any they missed.

The Bible has more than its share of barren wives who eventually bear uncommon children—Sarah's Isaac, Rebekah's Jacob, Elizabeth's John—and here, Hannah's Samuel. What's remarkable about her prayer for a child was (1) her promise, if she were to get pregnant, to give the child right back to God, and (2) what the priest's response to her silent prayers suggests about the spiritual state of Israel at that time: seeing her lips move but hearing no sound, he thought she came to the temple drunk. Hannah eventually delivered a boy—and delivered on her promise, too.

Ask:
- **How difficult was it to figure out all seven without looking at the sheets?**
- **What would have made it easier?**
- **How did you do at listening?**

Getting the Point

Talking to God

Ask kids these questions about talking to God:
- **What's prayer?**
- **How often do you pray?**
- **What do you pray about?**
- **Why should we pray?**
- **Is it ever hard to talk to God when you can't see him? Why or why not?**
- **What was the last thing you prayed about?**

> ### You'll need—
> - *a chalkboard, whiteboard, overhead projector, or a big piece of paper on the wall*
> - *copies of Three Things Ya Gotta Know about Prayer (page 23)*
> - *pens or pencils*

Now distribute copies of **Three Things Ya Gotta Know about Prayer** (page 23) along with a pen or pencil to each student. Ask them not to mutilate the sheets but to use them as an outline for what you're going to talk about.

Now say something like this: One reason it's hard for people to pray is that they have a whole bunch of wrong ideas about prayer. We're going to look briefly at three of those wrong ideas. Unscramble the letters in the words of the first question on your sheets, and tell me what the question says. [Unscrambled, the question says, *Where should I pray, and how should I position myself?*]

Ask your kids if they've ever thought that in order for their prayers to work, they needed to pray in a certain place or kneel or bow or do some other thing with the position of their body. (They may answer yes, which would

be nice for your teaching purposes; or they may answer no in a tone of voice that says, "How stupid can you be?") Tell them that whether or not they've wonder this, lots of people don't understand they can talk to God whenever and wherever they want. Ask them to write PRAY ANYWHERE! in the blank under the first question, while you write it on your whiteboard, overhead, or high-tech-paper-on-the-wall.

Now ask them to unscramble the second question. It says, *Do I need to talk a certain way when I pray?*

Say: **Have you ever heard people pray using fancy words, words they would never use in their normal everyday language?** [Using a deep fake voice, give them an example.] **O, our powerful Lord and God in heaven. Thou art so omnipotent, we are but mere ants in your sight. Verily, we sayeth to you, have mercy on us, that we may live but another day.**

Explain how young teens often struggle with prayer because they've heard adults pray like that and they don't think they can do it. Have them fill in the blank below the second question with: JUST TALK NORMAL! (You write it, too.) Explain that God isn't interested in fancy language. He's interested in hearing what's on our hearts and minds.

Finally, ask them to unscramble the third question. It says, *Should I only talk about certain things or act a certain way?*

Say: **So many people come to God and pretend they're someone else. It's not that they actually take on another personality, but they talk to God as if he doesn't know them. And they think they need to convince God they're good people or he won't listen. God is interested in you and he knows you! He longs to have a relationship with you, and that has to involve talking together. That's prayer!**

Have them fill in the blank under the third question with: BE YOURSELF! Add this to the class list up front, too.

Finish this section by having students turn their sheets over or put them away. Turn off the projector, erase the whiteboard, or take down your list. Then ask them to repeat back to you the three things they gotta know about prayer.

FLASHBACK

Hanny, the Wannabe Nanny

Divide your group into clusters of four or five. Tell the kids they're going to take a look at one of the prayer heroes of the Bible: Hannah. Their task will be to read the story of Hannah and, as a group, rewrite it as a modern-day story. They can change facts about the story if they want to—even what Hannah was praying for; but they need to have the flow of the story remain the same. Make sure they understand they'll have about five minutes to complete the activity and one of the group members should write their retelling of the story down on paper.

Now have students turn in their Bibles to 1 Samuel 1:2-28 to read the original story with their teammates. Circulate among the groups to make sure they understand what they're supposed to be doing. If your group is full of normal junior highers, you'll hear some groups discussing Hannah, and others discussing everything from baseball to cartoons to some subject that causes them to giggle but you don't ever find out exactly what they're talking about.

After about five minutes, or when it seems most groups are finished, instruct them to wrap it up. Depending on the size of your group, have some or all of the teams read their modern story. Or consider collecting them and reading a few from up front.

Then ask:

• **What did you like about Hannah's story?**

• **Have you ever felt like Hannah? When?**

• **What do you think about Hannah's decision to give Samuel to the priest? Would you have done that? Could you have done that?**

• **What can we learn about prayer from Hannah?**

FAST FORWARD

Pray on!

Distribute copies of **My Prayer List** (page 24). Also give a pencil or pen to each kid (some of them should already have something to write with from the last exercise). Ask the kids to list 20 things they need to pray about. For some students this will be easy, but for others it could be difficult. If some of your kids are struggling, you might suggest some categories, with questions like these:

• **Are there things about school you need to talk to God about?**

• **Are there things about your family that need prayer?**

• **What about your friends? Do any of them need prayer?**

• **Not just your friends, but your relationships with your friends. Is there any tension that needs prayer?**

• **Do you have relatives or neighbors that need prayer?**

• **Do you have friends who don't know Christ?**

Now you have a choice to make in how you wrap up this lesson time. If you have a mature group, or if you have a good leader to student ratio (one to seven or better), consider breaking up into groups for prayer. Have students pray for three or four things on their lists with others praying along silently.

If you're doubtful that your group could handle this assignment—or if you're, like, the only adult in a room full of 87 junior highers (ooh, that's got to be a form of primitive torture in some cultures), have your kids spend some time in silent prayer, bringing their needs to God. Bring the prayer time to a close with your own prayer to God (out loud) on behalf of the students.

SPEAK AND LISTEN!

Reptile on the Loose
Version 1
The other day I went to a big department store. While I was there the strangest thing happened. A man started waving his arms, running around the store, and shouting, "I'm a crocodile! I'm a crocodile!" Four security guards had to wrestle him to the ground. After that I bought some green socks and paid for them with the money my Grandma gave me for my birthday.

Reptile on the Loose
Version 2
The other day I went to a big grocery store. While I was there the strangest thing happened. A kid started waving his arms, running around the store, and shouting, "I'm an alligator! I'm an alligator!" Three security guards had to wrestle him to the ground. After that I bought some green underwear and paid for them with the money my uncle gave me for Christmas.

They're Aliens, Not Us!
Version 1
The movie was totally weird! First, these big aliens came from the planet Korg. They loved to eat orange slushies and pancakes. They took 14 junior highers with them back to their planet. The aliens put the kids in a museum that looked like a big mansion so the kids didn't mind all that much.

They're Aliens, Not Us!
Version 2
The TV show was totally weird! First, these little tiny aliens came from the planet Karf. They loved to eat raspberry slushies and French toast. Then they took 40 junior highers with them back to their planet. The aliens put the kids in a museum that looked like a big school so the kids hated it.

Fried Fish
Version 1
My science teacher is totally wacked! The other day he took a live fish, a cod, and put it in a fish tank that had electricity running through it. He said it was to show us the effect of electricity on fish, like that's such an important point of knowledge! Anyway, then he gave us an essay quiz on it, and I wrote, "Duh, the fish got zapped!" and my teacher gave me an A.

Fried Fish
Version 2
My science teacher is totally goofy! A couple weeks ago he took a live fish, a halibut, and put it in a fish tank that had electricity running through it. He said it was to show us the importance of not using electrical appliances in the bathtub, like that's such an important point of knowledge! Anyway, then he gave us a full-on essay test about it, and I wrote, "I think someone should report you to the Humane Society!" and my teacher gave me a C.

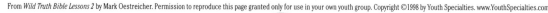

THREE THINGS YA GOTTA KNOW ABOUT PRAYER

1 Hewer oldush I rapy, nad who hulsod I sitpoion symelf?

＿ ＿ ＿ ＿ ＿   ＿ ＿ ＿ ＿ ＿ ＿   ＿   ＿ ＿ ＿ ＿ ，   ＿ ＿ ＿   ＿ ＿ ＿

＿ ＿ ＿ ＿ ＿   ＿ ＿ ＿ ＿ ＿ ＿ ＿   ＿ ＿ ＿ ＿ ＿ ？

Answer: Pray ＿＿＿＿＿＿！

2 Od I ened ot latk a tercain yaw hewn I yrap?

＿ ＿   ＿   ＿ ＿ ＿ ＿   ＿ ＿   ＿ ＿ ＿   ＿   ＿ ＿ ＿ ＿ ＿ ＿

＿ ＿ ＿   ＿ ＿ ＿ ＿   ＿   ＿ ＿ ＿ ＿ ？

Answer: ＿＿＿＿＿＿ talk ＿＿＿＿＿＿！

3. Housld I nlyo kalt bouta recitan hingst, ro tac a cretain yaw?

＿ ＿ ＿ ＿ ＿ ＿   ＿   ＿ ＿ ＿ ＿   ＿ ＿ ＿ ＿   ＿ ＿ ＿ ＿ ＿

＿ ＿ ＿ ＿ ＿ ＿   ＿ ＿ ＿ ＿ ＿ ， ＿ ＿   ＿ ＿ ＿   ＿

＿ ＿ ＿ ＿ ＿ ＿ ＿   ＿ ＿ ＿ ？

Answer: Be ＿＿＿＿＿＿＿＿＿！

MY PRAYER LIST

List 20 things you need to pray about. "Whoa! That's too many!" you say? C'mon, you can do it. Once you get started, the ideas will come faster and faster, and you'll be asking for more paper. There's nothing too small or too big for God to be interested in.

1. _____
2. _____
3. _____
4. _____
5. _____
6. _____
7. _____
8. _____
9. _____
10. _____
11. _____
12. _____
13. _____
14. _____
15. _____
16. _____
17. _____
18. _____
19. _____
20. _____

Joe's Bros the Sibling Sellers

Joseph's brothers, on responding when someone offends you

Bible passage: Genesis 37:1-28

GOALS

Students will—

- *Be able identify what it feels like to have another person offend them.*
- *Consider options for responding to an offense.*
- *Choose a plan of action for a current offense or a future offense.*

Important note: Don't tell your group the biblical subject of today's lesson. They'll have an opportunity to guess later.

JUMP START

You Offend Me!

Begin the time by asking your students what it means to offend another person. Hopefully, they'll know offending another person means to say or do something that is seen as an attack or affront to the other person's standards of conduct. Ask your kids if they've ever been offended. Ask a few to describe a recent incident of offense.

Realize, depending on your group, this discussion may or may not produce answers. Some kids, in the right group context, will be more than ready to talk about times they've been offended. Other students may not be willing to share. This sharing assumes a certain level of vulnerability. It's risky for kids to talk about offenses if there's a chance others will not fully accept them for their story. So play it by ear. A bunch of responses or no response at all will both set you up for the opening activity.

You'll need—
- *a sign that reads* I'M SO OFFENDED!
- *a sign that reads* NO OFFENSE TAKEN

Say: We're going to see if you can relate to some of these offenses. I'm going to read a list of items. I need you to respond with whether this event would offend you or not. If it would offend you, move toward the sign that says I'M SO OFFENDED! [point to the sign]. If it wouldn't offend you, move toward the sign that says NO OFFENSE TAKEN. [Make sure students don't just stay in their seats while you read the list. Encourage kids to have their own opinions and not to move where everyone else is moving.]

Then read this list:

- A friend talks about you behind your back. It's not mean but still not something all that complimentary.
- A friend brags to you about how she made it onto the soccer team you got cut from.
- Your mom tells you she's sure you can do better in school.
- You stand in the lunch line next to someone who obviously hasn't showered in days. He stinks.
- Your best friend can only invite one person to his or her birthday celebration at a great amusement park. You don't get invited.
- Your science teacher says all Christians are believers of fairy tales.
- Your brother drinks straight out of the milk carton.
- Your sister and you have a code—she doesn't tell on you and you don't tell on her. But today, she told your parents you drank straight out of the milk carton—something that bugs your mom.
- You invite a few friends over to watch a video.

In a family of 10 older brothers, a 17-year-old in Joseph's circumstances today probably wouldn't do much better. Baby of the family, his father's favorite, good looking, a bad habit of speaking before he thought. Every time Joseph opened his mouth around his 10 older brothers, he only reminded them of their own second-rate status in their father's eyes. The boy was probably unconscious of all the hatred he was stirring up, but his naiveté did him little good. His brothers started a string of events that—in quick succession—saw Joseph at the bottom of a dry well, behind a camel on a desert slave caravan, and in a foreign jail cell for attempted seduction of his employer's wife.

None of them accept.

- Your uncle belches loudly at the dinner table and says, "In some cultures that's considered a real compliment."
- You have a certain friend who, for every story you tell, always tops it with a bigger, better story.
- A friend asks you nicely to talk less. She says, "I don't mean to offend you, but you talk a lot."
- The lady you baby-sit for asks you to clean up the kitchen, but doesn't pay you any extra for doing it.
- You and your best friend have birthdays two days apart. You save up a bunch of money and buy your friend two CDs, a cool shirt, and a pen that records messages and plays them back. Your friend only gives you a card.

Now have students return to their seats and lead a short discussion on offenses with these questions:

- After hearing all those examples, do you have any more of your own to add?
- Are you a person who is easily offended or one who is hard to offend?
- What does it take to offend you?
- What's the difference between someone offending you and someone hurting you?
- What's are some ways to respond to offense? What makes a good response? What makes a poor response? Is the best response always to ignore it? [Not always, though often it is.]

GETTING THE POINT

It's All in the Response

Tell your group they'll be looking at some case studies—stories of junior highers who've been offended. They are to put themselves in the place of the central character of each story. Tell them they'll be asked to write a good response to the offense.

Say: There are a couple of big questions to ask yourself every time you feel offended.

First, did the other person mean to offend you? This answer is important for calculating your response. Second, are my feelings of offense a reflection of a real offense? Sometimes we take offense at things that aren't offensive. We're ticked at that person or feeling bad about ourselves, or there's some other reason that leads us to believe we're offended. Finally, and most importantly, what's my response going to be? If you can pause and consider your response, you find you end up regretting your actions less often.

Now distribute copies of **You Offend, I Respond** (page 29). Direct your students' attention to the first case study. Read it out loud to them, then ask them to write a good response individually or in pairs. Be careful—you might need to give

further instructions. If your group is filled with sixth-grade boys weaned on a steady diet of rip-your-opponent's-heart-out-and-show-it-to-him-while-it's-still-beating video games, they are more likely to come up with responses like, "Tear his head off and mail it to him fast enough that he can open the package before he dies." This, of course, runs counter to the intended goals of this lesson (duh!). So gauge your group. If they're fairly mature, don't give them excess guidance. If they squirm a lot, set some boundaries.

After they've had a minute to write their responses to the first case study, have a few kids share their answers. Then guide them through the second and third case studies in the same manner.

You'll need—
- *copies of You Offend, I Respond (page 29)*
- *pens or pencils*

José and his Loco Hermanos

Tell your students they're going to look at one more story of offense. This one they'll act out. Recruit actors for the following roles: José, José's father, José's brothers (Pepe, Juan, and Pedro), some chickens (one to four kids), some beans (one to four kids), and a traveling shoe salesman. You be the narrator (I've found from failed experience that having a student narrate a melodrama can make the whole thing sound more like a language learning repetition tape than world-class drama). Make sure the actors know they need to act out the story—ham it up as much as they can—as you read. Remind them that they volunteered for this role (unless they didn't volunteer, in which case you can remind them that you're a whole lot bigger than they are; unless you're not a whole lot bigger than they are, in which case you should remind them that you're asking nicely).

Now read the script (found on page 30). Pause long enough between actions for kids to play out their parts. Also pause for kids to repeat their lines, in character, after you read them.

After you finish the melodrama, have everyone give a hand to the actors. You might want to point out the Academy Award-winning performance of the beans—sure to become a classic.

Now ask your group: Does anyone recognize this story? What is it?

You'll need—
- Bibles
- volunteer actors for the melodrama
- optional—props are not necessary, but some simple props will add to the experience, especially a sombrero—you can even staple a piece of colored construction paper into a cone-shape so José can wear it as a hat

Most kids who were raised within spitting distance of a church will recognize this as the story of Joseph and his brothers. If they recognize it, have a few students tell the story as they remember it; then have them turn in their Bibles as you read the real story. It's found in Genesis 37:1-28. If they don't recognize it, tell them it's a story that appears in the Bible; then turn to the real story and read it.

After reading the passage, ask these questions:

- Would Joseph have been an easy little brother to get along with?

- If you were one of the brothers, how would you have felt when Joseph was given the coat of many colors by your father? What would you have done?

- If you were one of the brothers, how would you have felt when Joseph told you about his dream? What would you have done?

- What other responses could the brothers have chosen?

- If you were a friend of the brothers and they asked you for advice, what would you suggest they do?

What Will I Do?

Distribute copies of **What Will I Do?** (page 32) to each student. They should still have pens or pencils from earlier use.

Ask them to complete either the top section or the bottom section. The top section is an opportunity to process a good response to a current offense. If kids can't think of a current offense, the bottom section allows them the opportunity to make a commitment to a

You'll need—
- copies of *What Will I Do?* (page 32)
- pens or pencils

good response when someone offends them in the future.

Give the group a few minutes to write their answers, then have several of them share their responses. If you have time, consider having other members of the group give feedback on the individual responses.

Be sure to close your time in prayer, asking God to give all of you the courage to respond with his love when people offend us.

You Offend, I Respond

Singing the Blues

You've been on the basketball team for two years, playing forward. You're probably the second-best player. The best player on the team, Chris, is the other forward. Together, the two of you make a fearsome twosome, and your team is almost undefeated. You've started every game for two years straight. Your friendship with Chris is helping the team because you can anticipate each other's moves.

All this hit a major speed bump, however, three weeks ago, when *the other* Chris came to your school. And *the other* Chris is even better than the regular old Chris. *The other* Chris immediately joined your team and began competing for your starting spot. Everyone's talking about "the two Chrises." Two Chrises. You can hardly believe it. Today the coach had your friend Chris and another kid pick teams for a scrimmage game. Chris picked *the other* Chris—not you!

Your response:

Doggie Do

Old Mrs. Fairfield has had you walk her dog twice a week for a few months. She pays you a little. But the money is such a small amount that you consider it just a nice thing to do for her. She insists on paying you, so you take it rather than argue with her. You've never missed a scheduled walk. Every Monday and Thursday afternoon. She was a sweet old lady, and you were glad to help her.

But last week she told you she didn't need you to walk Puddles any more. You were a little confused, but figured she had other plans. Until today, when another old lady in the neighborhood told your mom that Mrs. Fairfield dropped you because you were "price-gouging her like a bandit—taking way too much money for way too little work."

Your response:

Friend or Foe?

You're the new kid in this school, moving from half an hour away. It's tough breaking into a new school, but you think you've found a group of friends to hang with. They're even a fairly popular group on campus, and frankly, you're a little surprised they've chosen to include you.

But today your world came crashing down. Someone you didn't even know handed you a note in the hallway. When you got to your history class, you opened it and read it. It said that the your new group of "friends" had a bet among themselves to see who would give away their secret first. The secret was that none of them could stand you—they were letting you hang around them for the fun of this little contest. The girls were convinced that the boys would crack and reveal the secret first. And the guys were betting that the girls would give it away first. Whoever told first had to buy Cokes for the others.

Your response:

José and His Loco Hermanos

Characters
- José
- José's father
- Pepe, Juan, and Pedro, José's brothers
- chickens (one to four)
- beans (one to four)
- traveling shoe salesman

José lived in the Mexican countryside with his dad and three older brothers, Pepe, Juan, and Pedro. Being the youngest kid, he'd often been a little spoiled.

One day José was walking through the house singing a little song he made up with the words "I'm a pretty nifty kid." *(pause and make sure José actually makes up a little song with those words)* He sang the song over and over to himself as he skipped through the house. His dad came in and gave him a huge bear hug, lifting him right off the ground. This was pretty amazing since his dad was old. José's dad said, "José, my wonderful and handsome son, you have found great favor in my eyes. And today I want to give you a special gift."

At this point José's older brothers, Pepe, Juan, and Pedro walked into the room. José's dad said, "Oh good, I want you to see the special gift I have for José."

At this, José's dad pulled out a sombrero and put it on José's head. But it wasn't just any sombrero—it was a beautiful multicolored sombrero. All the sons—José, Pepe, Juan, and Pedro—gasped in unison. The Sombrero of Many Colors was almost too beautiful.

Pepe said, "Father, do you have a Sombrero of Many Colors for me, too?"

José's father simply said, "No." This caused Pepe, Juan, and Pedro to begin whining and complaining. This whining and complaining went on and on.

José was proud of his Sombrero of Many Colors and circled around his whining brothers, singing, "Now I'm a pretty nifty kid with a Sombrero of

Many Colors." He sang this over and over again while dancing around his whining brothers.

A few days later, José asked his brothers to come see him. When they came in the room, José said, "I've had a dream I should tell you about." Pepe, Juan, and Pedro looked at each other, shrugged their shoulders, and said, "Okay."

José spoke: "In my dream, I had a chicken, and you all had chickens." *(pause at this point and have the chickens take their places on the side of the stage to act out the dream)* "All our chickens were strutting around and clucking. Then all your chickens bowed down to my chicken." The brothers didn't like the dream and started getting upset.

José continued, "Then there were these beans. I had a bean, and each of you had a bean. And the beans were sitting around doing whatever beans do. *(pause and expect your bean-actors to come up with something)* Then your beans bowed down to my bean."

The three brothers didn't like this dream because they knew it meant that they would bow down to José.

Later, when José was out of the room *(and all the chickens and beans were gone, too)*, José's brothers met to talk. They were nervous and kept looking over their shoulders to make sure no one was listening to them.

Pedro said, "I'm sick of this! No more super sombreros and bowing beans. Let's kill him!" Juan, who never had a thought of his own, said, "Yeah, let's do that."

Pepe, however, knew that it would bum out their father if José died, so he suggested, "How about if we sell him as a slave?"

Juan said, "Yeah, let's do that."

Pedro countered with, "I don't know, I still think we should kill him."

Juan said, "Yeah, let's do that."

Pepe came back with, "I think it would be better if we sold him. Then we'd get rid of him and make money, too!"

Juan said, "Yeah, let's do that."

Eventually Pepe won, and they tied up José and sold him to a traveling shoe salesman who was passing their house.

The traveling shoe salesman picked up José and carried him off.

WHAT WILL I Do?

Dealing with a current offense

1. Describe a way someone has offended you that you're still wrestling with.

2. What options do you have for responding to the offense?

3. What's the best response?

Choosing a response for the future

4. What are some of the ways you respond to offenses?

5. In general, what do you think is the best way to respond to offenses?

6. Will you commit to trying the best response next time?

❏ Yes   ❏ No

Hard-Knocks Pablo

Paul, on persecution and hardships

Bible passage: 2 Corinthians 11:23-27

Students will—

• *Understand what it means to suffer for their faith.*

• *Learn about Christian suffering around the world.*

• *Choose a response for persecution.*

JUMP START

I've Been Squashed, Smashed, Stomped, and Smushed

If your group has a dozen or less kids, have them stand in a circle. If you have more than that, divide them up into groups of six to 12 each (closer to 12 is better, but do what ya gotta do), and have these groups form circles.

You'll need—
• *no materials*

Ask one person from each group to stand in the middle and bend his or her knees a little bit (their knees shouldn't be locked). Now ask the rest of the kids to put one hand each on the center person's shoulders or head. Of course, lots of giggles and other various young teen-common sounds will volley through the room at this point. Depending on your comfort and familiarity level with your group, you might want to joke about this to diffuse it.

Say something like this: Don't get weird about this hands-on thing! The giggles I hear suggest a few of you find this *very* interesting!

Tell your kids that when you give the signal, those around the outside of the circle should try to push down on the center person, forcing him bend his legs more. At the same time the center person should try not to bend his legs any more than the small amount they're already bent.

Give this a few rounds, allowing different people to stand in the middle. Then, after the ambulances leave to rush kids to the hospital for emergency knee replacement surgery, invite the rest of the students back to their seats.

Ask these questions:

• **Was it difficult to stand without bending in the middle?** [Debrief their yes or no answers.]

• **Was it hard or easy to push the people in the middle down?** [Again, don't stop with simple yes or no answers.]

• **Now, slightly changing the subject, what is persecution?** [Making fun of someone or limiting them in some way because of who they are or what they believe.]

• **How does persecution work?**

• **Have you ever seen or heard of Christians being persecuted?** [Have a couple kids describe stories.]

• **Have you ever been persecuted?** [Have a couple kids tell their stories.]

GETTING THE POINT

The Real World

The Real World (page 36) includes four real-life, current stories of Christian persecution. All of them

You'll need—
• *one copy of **The Real World** (page 36) for you to read out loud or copies for everyone*

Broken bones, beat-up faces, and minor concussions that Evel Knievel and Dick Butkus endured were nothing but split lips compared to what the apostle named Paul lived through and eventually died from. And he slogged through such punishment not for professional compensation, either, but for the privilege of it. Observers then, as today, wondered about the emotional stability of a man who put himself deliberately and continually in harm's way. Paul just shrugged it off. Hey, it comes with the territory, he said. When you serve the King, you live—and may die—with trouble like this. But it's nothing compared to what the King's prepared for us when all the suffering is over.

are verifiable. But, just so you know, the real people depicted in these stories did not write them. The stories are written in the first person to help kids better relate to the characters. Set up this part of the lesson time by telling your students that persecution

of Christians is on the rise in our world today. There was lots of persecution in Bible times, and there's still a lot today. Explain that you're going to read four true stories of people who are being persecuted for their faith.

After you read the stories, ask:

• **How did these stories make you feel?**

• **Which story impacted you the most? Why?**

• **What would you do if these stories were about you?**

• **How do you think the characters should respond?**

Splash and Thud

Say: This morning, I'm going to ask you all to be sound-effects technicians. Let's practice. I'll say a word or phrase, and you all make appropriate sound effects.

Have them practice making sound effects as a group with these words:

> *You'll need—*
> • *one copy of Splash and Thud (page 37)*
> • *copies of Pablo and the Tuff Stuff (page 38)*
> • *Bibles*
> • *pens or pencils*

• **rainstorm**
• **hockey match**
• **forest fire**
• **marshmallow fight** (this should be interesting)

Ask your kids what they know about Paul the

apostle. Let them answer with as many facts and stories about Paul's life as they know: for some groups, this will last approximately four nano-seconds (blank stares; mumbles of "Paul who?"). For other groups, especially those chock-full of wonderfully knowledgeable Christian school kids, you might learn a few things about Paul. After their well-churched, Bible-story-receptacle brain space is emptied of its Pauline contents, tell them you're going to read a story about Paul (**Splash and Thud**, page 37), and they as a group need to provide all the sound effects.

Now read the story of Paul (adapted from 2 Corinthians 11:23-27). Pause every time you see three dots (...). This is your cue that the group should be making sounds.

After reading the story, wrestle your kids back to some sense of order (that might be tricky after they've thought up sound effects for *naked*), and have them turn to 2 Corinthians 11:23-27 in their Bibles. Ask them to read the passage to themselves as you distribute copies of the quiz **Pablo and the Tuff Stuff** (page

A little warning here that readers with years of junior high experience have already thought of. Some portions of your group, especially sixth-grade boys, may struggle with making the correct sound effects, and "accidentally" slip into other types of sound effects, especially sound effects for a movie about boys and bathrooms. If this happens, you have three choices. If it's not too distracting, ignore it. If it's fairly distracting to the rest of the group, nicely ask the guys (it won't be girls) to stop. The third option is to heave a metal folding chair or some other large object at them. But this last option usually has negative repercussions, so use this only if you want to be relieved of your junior high ministry leadership responsibilities, receive psychiatric help, and experience correctional facilities first-hand. Okay, are you with me on this? Now read the story!

38) and pens or pencils. After everything's been distributed, ask your kids to take the quiz. Give kids a few minutes to work on their own.

Here are the answers for **Pablo and the Tuff Stuff:**

1. Boats crashing and sinking, lack of appropriate clothing, people chucking rocks at him, tummy growling, lack of sleepy-weepy, floating around the sea, lots o' whippings, tossed into jail, almost died, smacked about with sticks, and icicle cold!

2. A ton!

3. It's actually a good thing (even though it might not feel like it) when people persecute you or you experience hardship. It makes your faith stronger.

4. Sure, this stuff can be a drag. But to tell the truth, I actually enjoy it when I'm persecuted because it's a great opportunity for God's strength to shine through me.

After most of your kids seem finished, pull them back together and check their answers verbally.

FAST FORWARD

So What?

Begin your wrap-up by asking your students these application-oriented questions:

- Is it possible to respond to persecution like Paul suggests?
- How can you do it? How can you have the right attitude in the midst of problems?
- What are some common forms of persecution that a Christian junior higher might face?
- How will you try to react next time you experience persecution?

You'll need—
- *one copy of* **Help Me!** *(page 39)*

Ask your students to give advice to some imaginary junior highers who are experiencing persecution and hardship. Read the three stories on page 39, then ask your group to respond orally.

Close your session with prayer, asking God to give everyone strength and courage to respond to persecution in ways that will build our faith.

THE REAL WORLD
four real-life stories of persecution

Everyone Is "Christian" in Denmark

Hi! My name is Malena, and I live in Denmark. It's a beautiful country, and I'm proud to be Danish. But it's kind of weird to be a Christian here. You see, Christianity is the national religion here. In other words, the government works with a certain denomination—called the State Church—and religion is loosely a part of most of what's done here.

So most people born in this country are baptized in a church, are members of churches, and consider themselves Christian. But few actually are Christians. Almost no one knows Jesus Christ or cares about living like a Christian.

In my school of 2,000 people, I don't know one other Christian. My church is small enough that I'm the only teenager. So I never ever get to hang out with other Christian teens. Everyone at my school calls me Sister Malena—like I'm a nun or something. And absolutely no one would be caught dead talking to me or being my friend—I'm that weird Jesus freak to everyone. It's pretty lonely.

Alone in Turkey

The country I live in has very, very few Christians. In fact, there are millions of people in Turkey and less than 1,000 Christians. My name is John, and I live in a city of 500,000 people. A grand total of four Christians live in my city—me and three others! Almost everyone else is Muslim. And because there are so many Muslims, it's not acceptable to be a Christian.

When people write us from where we used to live in California, they have to be careful not to mention Jesus or Christianity or our missions work. Often our mail is read by government officials before it gets to us. We could get into lots of trouble—probably kicked out of the country—if they found out about our work here (we're missionaries).

Imprisoned in China

My name is Moses (really, it is). I'm a pastor in China, and I was in charge of 700 churches. I start-ed a training center for leaders. We had 12 leaders in training and only one Bible for all of us to share.

The communist leaders found out about my work and put me in prison. My cell was 20-feet square and had 30 men in it. We had to sleep on our sides like sardines, and the toilet was a hole in the corner. The situation was so awful, but I'd do it again in a second because the Lord came so close to me during that time. I found myself singing constantly. Other prisoners asked me to teach them the songs I was singing, and before I knew it, 20 of them had decided to follow Jesus.

Stuck in Bethlehem

My story's a little different because the persecution isn't aimed directly at Christians, but the situation in my country is having a bad effect on the churches. My name is Lilli. I'm 12 years old, and I live in Bethlehem—you know, the place Jesus was born. There's a church about a mile from my house that marks the place Jesus came into the world.

My family has lived here for generations, hundreds and hundreds of years. But the problem is that my people, the Palestinians, and the people of Israel have had lots and lots of tensions for a long time now (longer than I've been alive). This wouldn't be a real big deal if it weren't for the fact that the Palestinians and Israelis share the same land. Recently, Israel gave us Bethlehem and seven other cities to be our own Palestinian territories.

The problem is we can't leave Bethlehem without permits, and they're hard to get. So my family, who has lived here for hundreds of years, can't leave the town limits. And except for the neat spiritual importance of Bethlehem, there's not a lot here. Lots of people in the church are giving up and moving to other countries where they'll have more freedom. The result is that our churches are shrinking and shrinking. People are saying that within 20 years there might not be any Christians left. That makes me sad.

SPLASH AND THUD

an adaptation of 2 Corinthians 11:23-27, for use with sound effects

Hey, I'm Paul! Maybe you've heard of me. I'm the guy who used to kill Christians...Then one day I was walking down a road...and this really, really, bright light toasted my eyesight...I fell to my knees...and had an encounter with Jesus himself. Ever since that time, I've been working to spread the good news about Jesus and the salvation he offers.

I've traveled a whole lot, too. I've walked all over the place...I've ridden on horses...and donkeys...I've been on small boats...and big ships...And in the process, I've received a bit of persecution. Here are a few of the things that have happened to me.

I've been arrested...and put in prison...a bunch of times. Usually, they put chains on my ankles and wrists...But you know what? Even when I was in prison, I sang Christian songs all the time...It drove some of the guards up a wall—but it made a big impression on some of the others. I've also been beaten on more than one occasion...In fact, I've almost died several times...See, someone skilled in abuse and torture decided that 40 whips with the wicked cat-of-nine-tails thing will kill you. So they whipped me 39 times...

A few times, I was beaten with long metal rods...

And once, a group of people gathered around me and threw stones at me...It was supposed to kill me, but God helped me get through it.

Three different times I was on a ship that crashed...One of those times, I floated around on a piece of wood for a whole day and a night...

I've almost died crossing rivers...

I've had bandits rob and beat me...

I've had nights when I didn't get any sleep at all...And days when I haven't had anything to drink...or eat...

Finally, I've had times when I've been freezing...and naked...

PABLO AND THE TUFF STUFF

1. Check the types of persecution and hardship Pablo endured.

❏ girls pinching his arms
❏ people calling him *salvation boy*
❏ boats crashing and sinking
❏ floating around the sea
❏ pizza with sauce gone bad
❏ lots o' whippings
❏ toothpicks jammed under his fingernails
❏ jail
❏ lack of appropriate clothing
❏ near-death (bummer!)
❏ people chucking rocks at him
❏ being the target for the rotten tomato throw while he was preaching

❏ tummy growling
❏ super megathirst
❏ KICK ME sign taped to his back
❏ science teachers telling him he's dumb
❏ smacked about with sticks
❏ lack of sleepy-weepy
❏ icicle cold!
❏ big ol' lions to fight with his bare hands
❏ forced to sing the national anthem in front of the entire Colosseum
❏ JESUS FREAK sign taped on his front door

2. Place a mark on the scale to show how much persecution and hardship Pablo went through in the name of Jesus Christ.

Nuthin'—what a wimp!   Yeah, some, I guess   Wow! A ton!

3. Read James 1:2 (That's right! Open your Bible and read it. That's how you'll know the answer to the question.) What is James saying about persecution and hardships?
❏ It totally stinks, and we should avoid it at all costs.
❏ When someone persecutes you, lash out and call them all sorts of mean ugly names. That'll show 'em.
❏ It's actually a good thing (even though it might not feel like it) when people persecute you or you experience hardship. It makes your faith stronger!
❏ Good Christians should never experience persecution.

4. Read 2 Corinthians 12:10. (Yeah, another verse! You can handle it!) What's Pablo saying about all his hardships and persecution?
❏ I wish they would stop (whine, whine, sniff, sniff).
❏ I can't complain really. I've experienced a bit of persecution. But God's given me lots and lots of money and cool cars. So it's okay.
❏ Beat me! C'mon! Is that all you've got?! I love it when you hurt me!
❏ Sure, some of this stuff is a drag sometimes. But to tell the truth, I actually enjoy it when I'm persecuted because it's a great opportunity for God's strength to shine through me.

Help Me!

three fictional case studies asking for advice

STEPHANIE

My life rots! I mean it. I don't experience any persecution but because my family has chosen to follow Jesus, our life sure is hard. First of all, when me and my mom and dad became Christians a few years ago, everyone in our extended family stopped talking to us. That hurts because I love and miss my grandparents and aunts and uncles and cousins. Then, because my dad refused to lie about something at work, his boss fired him. So my dad's been unemployed for two years and is having a hard time finding a job because he got fired.

So we've got no support from family, and we've got no money at all. And then, the final straw, last week the people in our church all had a big fight. And now the church is splitting. The few friends I have are going with the people who believe the other side is right.

What should I do? I want to believe that God cares—but it sure doesn't feel like it!

JESUS

My name is Jesus (it's a Spanish name—you say "Hey-Soos"), and my family and I come from Mexico. We've been Catholic all my life, but I learned about salvation a few years ago. Jesus is a common name in Mexico. But where I live now, no one knows that.

At school kids tease me all the time about my name. I might be able to blow it off if I didn't actually want to be a follower of the real Jesus. But I feel like they're making fun of him as much as they're making fun of me. Then, to make matters worse, no one at my church understands (there aren't many Mexicans around here) why I'm named Jesus. It's like my parents named me God or something. So they all treat me weird and never say my name. I don't want to change my name.

What should I do?

KIRK

My life changed two weeks ago. I've been a Christian ever since I can remember. But not many people outside of my family and my church knew that until two weeks ago. Two things happened in one day at school.

First, I decided to be kinda bold and give a speech in my English class about my relationship with God. The speech wasn't until fifth period. I was a little nervous but really pumped up too. So in third period when my science teacher started slamming the idea of creation, I spoke up and talked about my belief in God. I explained how I believed that God created the world and all of us.

I know there are other kids in my class who believe the same thing. But I guess they were too freaked, because when the teacher started snickering at me, the whole class broke out into laughter. Then I gave my speech a few hours later, and by the end of the day, the whole school was talking about the preacher-boy. Now no one—I mean it, absolutely no one—will talk to me at school. It's like I have some awful disease or something.

What should I do?

Andy & Sophie the King and Queen of Lies

Ananias & Sapphira, on lying

Bible passage: Acts 4:32-5:11

ANDY & SOPHIE

GOALS

Students will—

- *Explore the motives of and pressures behind lying, whether by them or by their peers.*
- *Understand the consequences of lying.*
- *Give advice to some imaginary junior highers who are struggling with lying and reflect on current lying in their own lives.*

JUMP START

Liar, Liar, Pants on Fire

Divide your group of students into smaller groups of four or five. Each of these groups will be a team for the opening lie-detection competition. Distribute copies of **Liar, Liar, Pants on Fire** (page 44) to your students, along with one pen or pencil for each group.

Ask if they've ever seen supermarket tabloid papers (the cheap papers or magazines near the checkouts that have unbelievable stories in them). Ask if anyone can remember any of the headlines they've seen.

You'll need—
- *copies of **Liar, Liar, Pants on Fire** (page 44) for each hormonally influenced, squirrel-like, not-a-kid-yet-not-an-adult student in your group*
- *one pen or pencil for each group of four or five*

Then say: On this sheet I passed out to you are a bunch of headlines from a tabloid called *The Weekly World News*, one of the most unbelievable of the whole bunch. In each grouping you see there are four headlines. Three of them are real headlines from *The Weekly World News* and one of them is a fake. Your job, as a group, is to decide on the fakes. Have one person from your group check one headline in each group that the majority of you

think is fake. In a couple of minutes, I'll give you the correct answers.

Give your kids about six or seven minutes to complete their task. Circulate among them to make sure they understand what they're supposed to be doing (some clueless group of boys will undoubtedly circle all the headlines under the assumption that all of them are unbelievable).

The headlines this author made up that never appeared in *The Weekly World News* (meaning the correct answers) are:

- New York landlord evicts tenant for keeping flock of 50 chickens in his apartment.
- Leading biologist crosses peacock and rhino—offspring looks like a flying chihuahua.
- Frisky feline claws through wall after owner leaves town.
- Ten people die in new-improved Chips Ahoy! taste test.
- Man gives birth to triplets in the back of a taxicab.

---

his severe story spotlights a particular kind of lying. Ananias and Sapphira let on to the church that they were giving all the money from a real estate sale to the church. It's not what they necessarily said that got them in hot water, but what they didn't say. They posed, they pretended, they were not forthcoming among a unique collection of people whose very survival as a church depended on integrity, honesty, transparency, and confession.

GETTING THE POINT

I Never Lie!

Keep the kids in their groups from the last activity and have them brainstorm what junior highers might lie about. Have each group create its own list; one person writes down the answers on the back of **Liar, Liar, Pants on Fire**.

After a few minutes, ask the groups to share their lists (if you've got a large junior high group—and therefore lots of these little groups—have three or four groups share their lists). As they share, try to write down the major categories on your overhead, poster board, or whiteboard.

Then ask these questions:

• **Why do people lie?**
• **Do junior highers lie more than elementary kids?** [Their answer will probably be a resounding yes]
• **Why do you think that is?**
• **You don't have to share it, but do you remember your last lie? Was it a little one or a big one?**
• **Do you think lying is ever okay? When?** [Most kids will answer yes to this. If they won't answer yes, it's probably because they know the answer is supposed to be no even though they think it's yes.]
• **If the answer is yes, what would make a lie okay? How do you find the line between lies that are okay and lies that are not?**
• **What do you think God thinks about lying?** [Here's a little hint: God is pure truth!]
• **When we lie, do you think it has any effect on our relationship with God?**
• **Are there any consequences to lying? If so, what might they be?** [Broken relationships, getting caught, getting in trouble, hurting other people, developing a habit of lying, other natural consequences.]

FLASHBACK

Will the Real Story Please Step Forward?

Tell your students that you're going to read a story to them. In fact, you're going to read them three short versions of the same story. It's a story that's in the Bible, which they may not be familiar with. Ask them to pay close attention, because you're going to ask them which version of the story they think is closest to the actual biblical account.

Then read the three versions of Andy and Sophie's story on **Will the Real Story Please Step Forward?** (page 45).

After you finish reading, have your students vote on which of the stories they think is the real Bible story. It's the second one, by the way. You didn't think Christmas pageants and potlucks were in the Bible, did you? But don't give away the correct answer. Let your students discover the answer as you read the real passage.

Have everyone turn in their Bibles to Acts 4:32-5:11. Read the passage out loud while they follow along.

Say:

• **What was the problem with Andy and Sophie's gift when they gave something that was worth so much?** [They lied.]
• **Why do you think the consequences were so severe?** [We don't know—but it shows us how much God hates lying.]

What You Should Do, What I Will Do

Say something like: You've all heard of "Dear Abby," right? Well, today, you're going to take her place and write some helpful advice to some young teens struggling with lying.

Distribute copies of **What You Should Do, What I Will Do** (page 46) and a pen or pencil to each kid. Some students will already have writing utensils from the opening exercise. Ask your students to read the three short Dear Abby letters and choose one to write a response for. Tell them clearly that their answers cannot be a simplistic just-stop-lying answer. Their advice needs to be constructive and helpful, the kind of advice they'd want if they were asking the question. Instruct them not to write on the bottom half of the paper at this time.

> **You'll need—**
> • copies of *What You Should Do, What I Will Do* (page 46)
> • *pens or pencils*

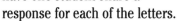
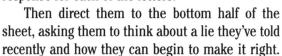

After they've finished writing their responses, have one student share a response for each of the letters.

Then direct them to the bottom half of the sheet, asking them to think about a lie they've told recently and how they can begin to make it right. Assure them you won't be having them share their answers.

After a few more minutes, close your time in prayer, asking God to give the kids courage to follow through on correcting the wrongs of their lies and for his power to resist lying and to live in truth and honesty.

Liar, Liar, Pants on Fire

Most of the following headlines were published in *The Weekly World News*. One headline in each group is a fake—it never appeared in *The Weekly World News* or any other paper. Find the fakes!

- ❏ Bride stood up in 1934 still waiting on the church steps.
- ❏ Baby born with mechanical heart.
- ❏ New York landlord evicts tenant for keeping flock of 50 chickens in his apartment.
- ❏ World War II bomber plane found on the moon.

- ❏ Leading biologist crosses peacock and rhino—offspring looks like a flying chihuahua.
- ❏ Sweet-toothed teen steals $80,000 of candy.
- ❏ Gorilla-lady captured!
- ❏ 2,500 year-old man found alive in coal mine.

- ❏ Cake in the face restores a man's sight.
- ❏ Boy eats angel-food cake and flies!
- ❏ Girl bursts into flames in shower! "All we found were wet ashes around the drain," say puzzled police.
- ❏ Frisky feline claws through wall after owner leaves town.

- ❏ "Elvis songs make cows give more milk," says farmer.
- ❏ Surgeon cuts out his own appendix in a traffic jam.
- ❏ Ten people die in new-improved Chips Ahoy! taste test.
- ❏ Bad haircut cost barber $1,000,000 in lawsuit.

- ❏ Man finds seven-foot boa constrictor around his toilet.
- ❏ Man gives birth to triplets in the back of a taxicab.
- ❏ Hero kid knocks out crook with water balloon.
- ❏ Chimp with human brain talks in German.

WILL THE REAL STORY PLEASE STEP FORWARD?

Read these three versions of Andy and Sophie's story (roughly taken from Acts 4:32-5:11), then have your students vote on the real story.

Andy and Sophie Fake the Potluck Casserole

Andy and Sophie were part of the first church. And a cool thing was happening: the people in the church were gathering for lunch every Sunday after church. It was the beginning of the traditional church potluck where each family would bring food items to share. Well, some of the people got fancy with their food trying to impress others.

Andy and Sophie were terrible about this. Every week they would bring something more fancy than they brought the week before. People would ooh and aah over the food. Andy and Sophie would make comments about how long it took them to make it.

All that stopped one Sunday when the caterer Andy and Sophie had been buying their fancy food from came as a visitor to the church. When people began oohing and aahing over the three-cheese succotash casserole Andy and Sophie had brought, he stepped forward and said, "I made it. They just bought it from me." Andy and Sophie tried to lie their way out of the mess, but everyone could plainly see the truth. Andy and Sophie continued attending the church but were never welcome at another potluck.

Andy and Sophie Drop Dead

Andy and Sophie were part of the first church. And a cool thing was happening: wealthier people in the church would occasionally sell a piece of land and give the money to the church. The money was used to help the poorer people so no one in the church had any unmet needs.

Andy and Sophie sold a piece of land and gave some of the money to the church. When the church leaders asked Andy if the money he'd given was everything he'd received from the sale of the land, he lied, and said, "Yup, that's all we got." The second Andy got the last word out of his mouth, he dropped dead on the floor with a big thunk!

Five minutes later, after Andy's body had been carried away, Sophie came into the room, not knowing what had happened to her husband. The church leaders asked her the same question, and she lied, too. She said, "Yeah, can you believe we didn't get any more for that gorgeous piece of property? Oh well, I hope the poor people are helped by our generous gift." As soon as the last word in her sentence slipped out of her mouth, Sophie's life slipped out of her body, and with a similar thunk, her dead body hit the floor.

Andy and Sophie Loose Their Good Seats for the Christmas Pageant

Andy and Sophie were part of the first church. And a cool thing was happening: the church was having its first Christmas pageant. They were going to act out the story of Jesus' birth, and they were using real sheep and stuff.

Tickets were sold to try to raise money for poor people in the church. Andy and Sophie wanted good seats but didn't want to pay that much. So they bribed the ticket salesperson with a goat and got the best seats in the house—right in the front row.

On the night of the performance, the ticket salesperson felt guilty about taking the goat as a bribe and confessed to some of the church leaders. The church leaders stopped the pageant after 10 minutes (the sheep were coming on stage) and asked Andy and Sophie to leave. It was humiliating for them, and they never returned to the church.

WHAT YOU SHOULD DO

Read these three letters and write an answer to one of them.

Dear Abby,
I'm caught in a lie and can't seems to get out. I told my best friend that I couldn't go to her birthday party because I had a rehearsal for my solo in our church youth choir musical. But I wanted to go to a movie with another friend. Now my best friend is asking how my solo is going and wants to come to the musical. I don't have a solo! What should I do?

—Solo-less in Seattle

Dear Abby,
I told my parents that I did all my homework for Math every week, but I was only doing about half of it. Today, my teacher sent home a progress report showing how many homework assignments I'd missed. My parents will be so mad and disappointed in me, too. The progress report has to be signed by my parents and returned by next week. What should I do?

—Scared in Sacramento

Dear Abby,
This string of lies is killing me. I told my youth pastor that I couldn't come to youth group because I had too much homework (which I didn't have). Then when she asked me how my homework load was, I lied again and said it was getting worse. Later, she called to see if she could take me out for a Coke, and because I felt so guilty, I said I couldn't because I was grounded. I keep lying and don't know how to stop. What should I do?

—Trapped in Toledo

Dear _____,

Here's what you should do:

Signing for Abby,

WHAT I WILL DO

Now, give some advice to yourself!

A lie I've told recently (you can use a few words or some code that only you would understand if you're worried about anyone seeing this):

What I'm going to do about this lie to begin to make it right this week:

Richie Rich the Material Boy

The rich young ruler, on materialism

Bible passage: Luke 18:18-27

Students will—

- *"Add it up" and consider their wealth.*
- *Analyze different results of materialism.*
- *Choose a position about materialism.*

JUMP START

They're Mine, All Mine

Begin your group time by distributing clothespins to your students (this will only work if the clothespins are the spring-mechanism style). Distribute the same amount to each kid—one each will work, more would be better. Ask them to clip the clothespins on the outside of their sleeves.

Explain that their goal will be to see how many clothespins they can get clipped on their own sleeves by the time three minutes is up. They can spin and move to get away from people, but they can't put their hands over their clothespins or push someone away. And the clothespins must remain on the outside of their sleeves—not in their pockets or under their armpits!

Have the kids stand up, and give them the signal to begin. Three minutes is a good length of time to let them play, but if the game looses steam—or starts to get out of control—stop it earlier. While you watch the clock, watch the kids, too—someone is bound to cheat, stashing stolen clothespins in some unimaginable place.

> *You'll need—*
> - *one or more spring-type clothespins for each student (about three per kid would be better)*

GETTING THE POINT

What I Want, What I Got, What They Got

Pass out copies of **What I Want** (page 50) and pens or pencils to each student. As you're distributing this stuff, tell the kids with a larger-than-life, excited, game-show-host voice that each of them have won $1,000,000. And they have three minutes to write down how they'll spend it. In order to spend it, they have to draw a picture of the items they'll spend it on and write an approximate cost next to each item. Now let them go wild!

After a few minutes, have a few students share some of the highlights of their lists. Then distribute **What I Got** (page 51) or have them turn the handout over, depending on how you copied the Wild Pages.

> *You'll need—*
> - *copies of **What I Want** (page 50) and **What I Got** (page 51)—copied back-to-back, if possible*
> - *pens or pencils*
> - *three copies of **What They Got** (page 52)*

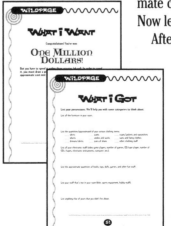

He wasn't just rich, but young as well. The combination says a lot about him—ambitious, bright, a Details subscriber. He knew how to leverage relationships as well as deals for the sake of a career climb that promised to be nothing less than stellar. Two homes, one of them on the bay where he kept a 32-foot sailboat…a modest collection of Harleys…horses with champion bloodlines that his money bought and his wife trained to relieve her days and nights of his absence. Meanwhile, he had been feeling a quiet, simmering anxiety about things himself. So when he walked out of the midtown restaurant and saw a street preacher, he waited until the sermon was done and the handful of listeners dispersed before posing his question. He wasn't ready for the answer.

Say something like this: Okay, now it's time for a little dose of reality. Certainly, some of you have more stuff than others of you. But my guess is, we all have more than we think we do. So take a few minutes and try to list everything you own on this page.

Roam around the room to check if kids understand the assignment. Of course, the quantity of stuff will vary from youth group to youth group depending on the socio-economic level of the people in your church. And some kids will have much more than others. But, unless you work in a somewhat impoverished area, this should produce surprising lists. If you *do* live in an impoverished area, this probably wouldn't be a good exercise. Let your kids do the **What I Got** sheet (page 51), then spend some time talking about how materialism isn't only an issue for people with lots of stuff—materialism is the desire for lots of stuff, and people without can fall into that trap also!

Pull your group back to attention after a few minutes, and ask for one boy and two girls who will read short stories. Explain that these are real stories of real junior highers. Then have the boy read Alex's story and the two girls read Raena's and Cassandra's stories (**What They Got**, page 52).

After they've read, ask these questions:

• How would you feel if you were one of these kids?

• What would these kids think if they walked into your home, into your room?

• What would you do if you were forced to switch places with one of them for a year?

• When you look at your list of stuff, then hear their stories, how do you feel about your stuff?

• What's materialism? [Officially, it's putting material things before anything else; but it might be easier for junior highers to understand something like this: materialism is focusing on possessions all the time, focusing on the stuff you have, and always wanting more.]

• Do you think you are materialistic? Why or why not?

• Our world—TV, movies, advertising—tells us materialism is great. What might not be good about it?

• What might be some of the negative consequences of materialism?

• Do you think God cares about materialism? Why or why not?

Richie Rich and His Screaming Wallet

Before your group time, recruit four students to read the parts in this reader's theater. Tell your students not to worry—it's not a drama that they have to act out. They only read their lines. Try to plan ahead enough to read through the script with the four readers two or three times so they're comfortable with their parts. Tell the Screaming Wallet to use a high-pitched, annoying voice and scream all the lines. It would be best if this person isn't visible. If you use a sound system, give the reader a mic that can be used from out of sight. Otherwise, the reader can crouch down so people don't notice "the wallet" during the reading. The other three characters simply stand side by side in front of the rest of the group.

You'll need—
• *four copies of Richie Rich and His Screaming Wallet (page 53)*
• *Bibles*

After the reading, ask your students to turn in their Bibles to Luke 18:18-27. Ask a student who reads well to read the passage or read it yourself while they follow along in their own Bibles.

Then ask:

- **What was Jesus really concerned about with this guy?** [His materialism—putting things before God.]

- **Did Jesus really want him to sell everything?** [Probably, but we don't know. We can be pretty sure that Jesus was testing him to see where his priorities were. It became obvious that his priority was his money.]

- **Why do you think the guy didn't do what Jesus asked?**

- **What would you have done if you were the rich young man?**

The Big Sell-out

Ask your students to look back at their copy of **What I Got** listing all their possessions. Hopefully, this sheet still exists as a fairly intact piece of paper. Of course, this is not always the case with junior highers and paper.

You'll need—
• *the students' completed* ***What I Got*** *Wild Pages*

A little warning: this final step will be more of a stretch for your kids than most of the final steps suggested in this book. Most applications ask them to talk to someone or pray or do something that does-n't cost them anything. This application has the guts, the audacity, to ask them to give up something—to give away some of their own stuff! *Proceed with caution.* And be willing to give an example of your own.

Here's the deal. Ask your kids to look over their lists of stuff and consider whether there's something on the list that they will give up. You're look-ing for one or two things that they will either give away or sell and give all the money to God. Ask them to pray silently for a minute, asking God to reveal to them something on their lists that would be good to give up. Make it clear that this is not a way of earning their way to heaven or anything magical. It's a way of telling God that he's more important than their material possessions. It's a way to fight materialism. You can even challenge them to take this seriously—choose something that they'll miss! The activity will mean more if the object they give up means more to them.

Ask those who want to participate to circle the one or two things they'll give away or sell this week. Share one thing you're going to give away or sell. Before you pray, challenge your kids to move away from materialism and to remember that stuff will never make them as happy as Jesus will.

Congratulations! You've won

One Million Dollars!

But you have to spend it within three minutes (oh-no!). In order to spend it, you must draw a picture of each item you want to buy and write an approximate cost next to it. Go! Hurry! Draw!

WHAT I GOT

List your possessions. We'll help you with some categories to think about.

List all the furniture in your room.

List the quantities (approximate) of your various clothing items:

____ shirts	____ pants	____ coats/jackets and sweatshirts
____ shorts	____ undies and socks	____ suits and fancy clothes
____ dresses/skirts	____ pairs of shoes	____ other clothing stuff

List all your electronic stuff (video game players, number of games, CD/tape player, number of CDs /tapes, electronic instruments, computer, etc.).

List the approximate quantities of books, toys, dolls, games, and other fun stuff.

List your stuff that's not in your room (bike, sports equipment, hobby stuff).

List anything else of yours that you didn't list above.

WHAT THEY GOT

three real-life, true stories of teens without much stuff

No Money, No Welfare

Hey. My name's Alex, and my family lives in the southern part of Bulgaria among the Gypsy people. After years and years of communism in my country, there are a lot of problems. Things are getting a little better, but the average salary in my country is still about $27 a month. But it's worse with the Gypsy people—90 percent of the people are unemployed.

So, as you can guess, no one in my family has a job. And we don't have welfare like you have in your country. We try to survive with absolutely no money. We plant vegetables in a field, and we work little odd jobs here and there. We never, ever get to buy anything like clothes or toys or especially furniture. I hope things will get better.

Thirteen in a Closet

Hi, I'm Raena, and I live with my mom and dad and 10 brothers and sisters in a colonia just south of the Texas border. A colonia is like a neighborhood. It's a part of a town or city—but the area is usually made up of houses that people kind of build out of any materials they can find.

I'm excited because last week my family got a new house! Some teenagers from the United States came and built it for us. It's pretty small, only eight feet wide and 12 feet long (about the size of a large closet in your house maybe), but it more than doubles our space. It's right next to our old house, so we can use them both. Now my parents and little brothers and sisters can stay in the old house, and me and the five older kids will stay in the new one.

We don't have any furniture or anything, so we're sleeping on the ground. But it sure is better than all 13 of us sleeping on the three beds in the old house.

Drugs, Noise, and a Hot Plate

I'm Cassandra, and I live in downtown Los Angeles. I live in a hotel. Now, that might sound nice to some of you, but I don't think you'd like it very much. Our hotel is full of drug dealers and users, prostitutes, and pimps. It's noisy at all times of the night, which makes it hard to sleep.

The room we live in—well, let's just say it's not the Holiday Inn! There's my mom and stepdad, my older sister and my younger brother, my Grandma, and my nephew. I'm not sure you understood—we all live in one room. There's no kitchen, so we cook our meals on a little hot plate, when we have meals, that is.

My stepdad's trying to find a job, but there aren't many around here. Once in a while we run totally out of money and have to live on the streets for a few nights until we get some more. I hope someday we can have a little apartment somewhere. I've never spent a night in a bed by myself.

Richie Rich and His Screaming Wallet

a reader's theater for four people

Characters

- Narrator
- Jesus
- Richie Rich
- Screaming Wallet (an off-stage voice)

NARRATOR: Jesus was teaching a bunch of people, and standing nearby, listening, was a very rich young man.

RICHIE: I'm a very rich young man.

JESUS: I'm teaching a bunch of people.

RICHIE: I'm a very rich young man.

NARRATOR: As the very rich young man—Richie Rich was his name—thought about how rich and young he was…

RICHIE: I'm really rich. And, you know what? I'm also a young man. That would make me a very rich young man.

NARRATOR: He decided to ask Jesus a question.

RICHIE: Excuse me…Mr. Jesus?

JESUS: Yes?

RICHIE: How can I get eternal life?

JESUS: Do you know about the commandments? You know…the big 10?

RICHIE: Yes I do. And I've kept every single one of them since I was a very rich young baby.

JESUS: Well then! There's only one more thing you have to do.

RICHIE: (eagerly) What's that?

JESUS: Sell everything you own and give the money to poor people.

SCREAMING WALLET AAAHHHHHHHHH!!!

NARRATOR: What was that?

JESUS: What was that?

RICHIE: That was…um…my wallet.

NARRATOR & JESUS: (in unison) Your wallet?

SCREAMING WALLET AAAHHHHHHHHHHH!!!!

RICHIE: Uh, yeah. My wallet gets a little bit freaked when anyone suggests I give a lot of money away.

SCREAMING WALLET AAAHHHHHHHHHHH!!! AAH! AAH! AAH!

NARRATOR: Can you make it stop?

JESUS: Can you please? It's driving me up a wall!

SCREAMING WALLET No! No! No! No giving away lots of money! No! No!

RICHIE: (hand on pocket, where wallet would be) I can't make it stop because it's saying what I'm thinking. I guess I'll leave now. (walks off stage with head down)

SCREAMING WALLET We're leaving now! Ha! No money for poor people!

JESUS: Wow. That was really annoying. I guess we know where his priorities are.

NARRATOR: So there you have it. Jesus knew the very rich young man was hyper about his money. He knew the man would never live totally for God because he would always put his money first. So he asked the very rich young man to give it up to see if he would be willing to give up everything for Christ as the Bible says. He wasn't. Bummer for him!

Roof Club the Extra-Mile Friends

The stretcher bearers who lowered their friend through a roof to Jesus, on meeting your friends' needs

Bible passage: Luke 5:18-26

Students will—

- *Learn how to look for their friends' needs.*
- *Understand the importance of meeting those needs.*
- *Make a plan to meet one need this week.*

JUMP START

The Friendship Challenge

Pass out copies of **The Friendship Challenge** (page 58) and a pen or pencil (or some other writing utensil—stick of lipstick, crayon, tube of white-out, etc.) to each student. Tell them not to begin the challenge until they've heard all the rules.

You'll need—
- *copies of The Friendship Challenge (page 58)*
- *pens or pencils*

Say: Here are the rules.

1. You can complete these items in any order you want.
2. You must get someone's initials (as many as the item asks for) to prove you completed it.
3. For items that call for you to get other people to help you, you can't always get together with the same people. Mix it up a bit!
4. You can only get a person's initials one time—all initialed items must be done by different people (for groups over 10) **or** you can get one person's initials only one or two times (for groups under 10).

5. When you finish, write your name on the top, and bring it to me. The first four people to do so win.

Now start the game. This will probably take your group about five minutes. You should only let the game continue until you have the first four completed forms in your hands. Then call off the game, and have students return to their seats. Announce the winners with showy fanfare. You may want to award some kind of small prize to the first-place winner—like, maybe, a trip to Europe or something.

After the mayhem has subsided, ask these questions:

- **How would you describe a friend?**
- **What are the characteristics of a good friend?**
- **What's the single-most important characteristic of a good friend?**
- **What's the worst thing a friend could do to you?**
- **How do junior highers go about getting friends?**

GETTING THE POINT

Need Watchers

Say something like this: One of the most important characteristics

You'll need—
- *one copy of Guess My Needs (page 59)*

For whatever reasons, there was no stopping the stretcher bearers. Maybe the paraplegic (or quadriplegic) had recruited a few strangers off the street with the offer of money. Maybe he had nagged his roommates until they finally gave in just to shut him up, and took him to the upcountry healer who was rumored to be in the neighborhood. Most likely, though, it was deep, empathetic friendship that propelled the stretcher bearers to the house where Jesus was, up to the roof when the crowd wouldn't give way, and—in a burst of ingenuity or desperation—through the roof and down to the floor where Jesus stood. At this point, St. Luke reports an intriguing detail about the friends and the paraplegic: Jesus saw *their* faith, then forgave *his* sins.

of being a good friend—and the whole point of our time today—is recognizing the needs of your friends and trying to meet those needs. **How can you recognize the needs a friend might have?** [Listen a lot; look for clues that a need exists; get to know your friend.]

Now tell your group you're going to give them a little practice at spotting needs. Tell them you're going to read some stories about some junior highers, and they'll have the assignment of figuring out the character's needs. Explain that you realize this might be a little unrealistic since they don't know the characters.

The stories from **Guess My Needs** (page 59) are arranged so that you can read them in sections. The first section doesn't reveal much about the real need at all—there are hints about it. The second section begins to reveal the need a little more clearly, and the third section almost comes right out and says it. This simulates the levels of intimacy in a friendship. Some kids never get past a superficial friendship level with their friends, which makes it difficult to spot needs. After reading each section, stop and give kids the opportunity to offer their opinions on what the character's needs are.

After you finish all three stories, point to one wall and declare it the I-wouldn't-lift-a-finger-for-my-friends wall. Then point to the opposite wall and declare it the I-would-go-to-extreme-lengths-to-help-meet-my-friends-needs wall.

Now ask your kids to stand up and move to one wall or the other or somewhere in between to show their answers to the question: **How extreme will you be in meeting your friends needs?**

The Roof Club

If your group has more than 10 kids in it, divide it into groups of about six or seven. (Yeah, I know that math doesn't add up. About seven kids per group would be the ideal size, okay? It would be *really* ideal if you had an adult leader for every group.)

You'll need—
• *Bibles*

If your group has more than 35, you'll want to use groups that are closer to 10 in size. If your group is over 70, you'll never make it through seven dramas so consider making the groups around 15 in size and don't require everyone in the group to be active in the drama.

Ask the groups to read Luke 5:18-26 and come up with a modern-day retelling of that story. Tell them they'll have about five or six minutes to come up with the drama. You should roam around to the different groups (especially if you don't have other adults in them) and offer a little help and direction.

After about six minutes or when most of the groups seem to be done (they may need extra time), have the groups come up one at a time and perform their dramas. Make sure you wildly praise each group for their efforts—if they exert any effort at all.

After all the groups are finished, ask:

• **How extreme were the actions of the friends?** [Massively extreme! It was no more appropriate to rip a hole in someone's roof in Jesus' time than it would be today.]

• **What do you think gave the friends the courage to take such radical action?** [They believed that Jesus could heal their friend.]

• **What was the reason Jesus gave for why he would heal the guy?** [The faith of the friends! This is an important point. The text doesn't say anything about the faith of the crippled man—he may or may not have had faith. But Jesus says he will heal the man because of the faith of the friends.]

Say something like this: We can have a big impact on our friends with our faith. The example of this story teaches us that 1) we need to recognize our friends' needs and bring them to God in prayer with faith, and 2) God, in some way and at some time, will respond to our faith.

I'll Meet That Need!

Pass out **I'll Meet That Need!** (page 60) to your kids. They should already have pens or pencils from the opening exercise. By now they've probably left permanent markings on the students on both sides of them. If they were using pencils, the points have been broken off (but there should be lots of little lead bits being ground into your carpeting or tile. Okay, I'll move on.)

Tell your kids it's time to get personal—time to apply all this understanding about meeting friends' needs to their own lives.

The Wild Page is self-explanatory—fill out the questions, creating a plan of action for meeting one specific need of a friend. Give them about four minutes to work, then ask if a few will share their answers out loud.

If you have time, it would be great to divide your group into clusters of three or four and have them pray for each other—that God would help them follow through on meeting their friends' needs. If you don't have time for this, ask two or three students to pray for the whole group.

You'll need—
• copies of *I'll Meet That Need!* (page 60), cut in half
• pens or pencils

THE FRIENDSHIP CHALLENGE

Complete these items in any order you choose. But you must get someone's initials in the blank next to the item to confirm it.

1. Get two other people with you and sing the Michael W. Smith song, "Friends," while you have your arms around each other's shoulders:

Friends are friends forever, if the Lord's the Lord of them.
And a friend will not say never, 'cause the welcome will not end.
Though it's hard to let you go, in the Father's hands we know,
That a lifetime's not too long, to live as friends.

If you don't know the tune, make one up!
  Have your two cosigners initial here:

_____

_____

2. Stand on a chair and yell in a big-time, whiny, begging voice, **"Won't you please be my friend?"**
  Have someone who heard you initial here:

_____

3. Get two other people and form a circle holding hands. Skip around while chanting this little word of advice:
You can pick your friends,
And you can pick your nose,
But you can't pick your friend's nose.
  Have those two sick people initial here:

_____

_____

4. Get with one other person. Stand side by side. One of you should shout, **"A FRIEND IS..."** and the other person should shout a word that completes the sentence. You have to do this five times, taking turns and making up different endings to the sentence each time.
  Have your buddy initial here:

_____

5. Grab someone and have them sit on a chair in front of you while you stand. Preach this mini-sermon to your one-person audience (use your best TV preacher voice):
In the book of Proverbs, the author makes an important observation about friendship. He writes, "A friend sticketh closer than a brother." So today, I challenge you to stick. Amen.
  Have your audience initial here (then let him or her preach to you):

_____

6. Get two other people and lead them in a cheer.

You shout: *Give me an F!*	They shout: *F!*
You shout: *Give me an R!*	They shout: *R!*
You shout: *Give me an I!*	They shout: *I!*
You shout: *Give me an E!*	They shout: *E!*
You shout: *Give me an N!*	They shout: *N!*
You shout: *Give me a D!*	They shout: *D!*
You shout: *What's that spell?*	They shout: *Friend!*
You shout: *What's that spell?*	They shout: *Friend!*

You: *What's that spell?*
Everyone shouts: *Friend! Friend! Friend! Whooooooo!*

  Have your two cheer partners initial here (and initial their sheets also):

_____

_____

GUESS MY NEEDS

Read these three stories one section at a time, asking your students to identify the needs of the main character. The answers are at the end of each story, so *don't make copies* of this page for your students.

Jenny

You've been hanging around Jenny for a few weeks at school. She's fun to be with but occasionally gets moody. When she gets this way, she's difficult to be around.

What might be Jenny's need? [Pause for student responses.]

Yesterday, you went over to Jenny's house for the first time. She was in one of those moods. You noticed something that you hadn't noticed before—Jenny was wearing the same outfit she'd had on the day before.

What might be Jenny's need? [Pause for student responses.]

Now that you've noticed this wearing-the-same-clothes thing, you start to pay a little more attention. And you realize that Jenny only has one pair of jeans and a few shirts. And she seems to get in a mood when people talk about clothes.

What might be Jenny's need? [Pause for student responses. Jenny's family probably doesn't have enough money to buy her more clothes.]

What could you do to meet her need? [Pause for student responses. Consider buying her some clothes or giving her some of yours.]

Yoshi

You've known Yoshi for about six months, ever since he and his mom moved to your town. The two of you have done a few things together, but you don't know him all that well. Sometimes he acts stupid and childish.

What might be Yoshi's need? [Pause for student responses.]

You start spending more time with Yoshi. You go over to his apartment sometimes after school and play video games. His mom is never there—she has to work long hours. So Yoshi's at home by himself all the time. He pretty much takes care of himself, cooking his own meals and doing his own laundry. Sometimes he seems responsible to you. He does so many adult things. But other times, he still acts like a little kid—all giggly and goofy.

What might be Yoshi's need? [Pause for student responses.]

You ask Yoshi over to your house for dinner one night. During the meal, he's quiet—not at all like you're used to seeing him. After dinner, in your room, you ask him why he was so quiet, and he answers: "I've never been with a family like that before. I guess I didn't know how to act."

What might be Yoshi's need? [Pause for student responses. Yoshi is probably lonely and acts like a little kid sometimes because he doesn't have any examples of how he should act.]

What could you do to meet his need? [Pause for student responses. Have Yoshi spend a lot more time with your family. Introduce him to some of your other friends. Invite him to church with you.]

Charles

You met Charles about a month ago when the two of you were assigned as partners for a science project. Charles is smart so you were happy about the assignment. Charles seems like he's got it all together. He's got some friends—not a whole bunch, but some—he does well in school, and he's got a nice family.

What might be Charles' need? [Pause for student responses.]

In the process of doing your science project, you and Charles hit it off and become friends. He's a nice guy. The only strange thing you've noticed is that he sometimes makes comments like "I don't understand you Christians" and "I swear, are you always happy?"

What might be Charles' need? [Pause for student responses.]

You decide to invite Charles to your youth group. His response is, "I don't know. That church stuff probably isn't for me. I've got my life pretty well together, you know?"

What might be Charles' need? [Pause for student responses. Charles needs Jesus!]

What could you do to meet his need? [Pause for student responses. Keep talking to Charles about God. Invite him to church again. Pray for him. Make sure you're real about your Christianity.]

WILDPAGE

I'll Meet That Need!

TIME TO GET PERSONAL!

Write the name of a friend that has a need you know about.

What is this friend's need?

How will you try to meet his or her need this week?

✂ -

WILDPAGE

I'll Meet That Need!

TIME TO GET PERSONAL!

Write the name of a friend that has a need you know about.

What is this friend's need?

How will you try to meet his or her need this week?

Hammerhead
the Nap-Time Monitor

Jael, on doing difficult things for God

Bible passage: Judges 4:17-22

GOALS

Students will—

- *Respond to difficult situation case studies.*
- *Identify difficult situations they or other young teens face.*
- *Choose a course of action for one difficult situation.*

JUMP START

For groups of 12 or more (see Modern Sculpture, next page, for less than 12):

The 10-Foot Pole

Clear a space at least 12-feet square (much more, of course, if you have a large group). If your group has between 12 and 20 students, have them work together as one team. If your group is larger than 20, split them into teams of 10 to 15 students each. Instruct the students that their goal is to build a tower, or a pole, of 10 feet. This is not a length of 10 feet, but 10 actual feet-with-toes of students, standing up on end, heal on toe, 10 high. The stack of feet needs to go straight up—not sideways or even leaning. Be careful of girls in dresses! Involve them in appropriate ways. Don't give them a whole lot more guidance than that initially. Let them begin to work together on this difficult task.

You'll need—
- *no materials*

If they stand around with glazed looks on their faces (I mean, more than usual), offer some suggestions. Keep your suggestions simple and general at first. Allow them to struggle for a while, but if they still seem clueless after a period of time, then give them more specific help.

Offer suggestions like these:

- **Consider using the feet of shorter people on the bottom of the pole.**
- **The people on the bottom of the pole could sit down and use both of their feet.**
- **Not everyone has to have a foot in the pole— some can help balance other people or even hold them.**
- **Taller people make great middle-of-the-stack choices because they can lift their legs higher than shorter people.**
- **Consider saving a light person to be lifted sideways to provide the top two feet.**

If the exercise is too simple for your group (they should struggle with this), then tell them the 10-foot pole was only the warm up. Now they need to do a 14-foot pole or a 16-foot pole (whatever would make the activity a challenge).

Once your group has accomplished this difficult task, give them gobs of praise for a job well done.

Then ask them these questions:

- **On a scale of one to 10, how difficult was this task?**
- **What made it difficult?**
- **What would have made it easier?**
- **How do you feel, in general about difficult tasks?**

Irony, coincidence, and the unexpected are as operative in war as in peace. Case in point: not long after Joshua's death, Israel is invaded and controlled by Jabin, a Canaanite king. After 20 years of occupation, the Israelis say enough's enough and revolt. Though Jabin sends his general Sisera to quell the uprising, his army is defeated and Sisera alone escapes with his life, fleeing to a nearby nomadic clan known for their alliance with Jabin. The woman of the house—Jael was her name—recognizes the general, gives him a bed, a tall drink, and promises to keep mum about his presence there. After he falls asleep, exhausted, the woman pins his head to the ground with a spike through his temples. Jael's nail. Maybe she remembered that, despite her husband's pact with Jabin, her clan's ancestry was directly related to the in-laws of Moses himself. Sometimes blood runs deeper than alliances.

For groups of less than 12 students:

Modern Sculpture

Clear an area at least 12-feet square, and have your students stand in the middle of it. Tell them they are going to make a modern sculpture with their bodies. First, let them use themselves to make some kind of modern sculpture together. The only rule for the first round is they all have to be connected somehow.

After they come up with something, give them a little harder challenge. Tell them for the second round, their modern sculpture can only have so many feet or hands touching the ground (touch points). For the second round, the number should be a little less than one touch point for each student. For instance, if you have 10 kids, the second round should be limited to about eight touch points. This should be fairly easy, because most of the kids can stand on one foot and couple can be on shoulders. They can't use any chairs, walls, or other items to prop themselves up.

You'll need—
• *no materials*

After they've completed the second round challenge, continue to make the activity more and more difficult by limiting the number of touch points. The goal is to give them a challenge that is difficult but doable. The number of touch points will depend on the size of the group as well as with their motivation to succeed. Theoretically, a group of 10 should be able to do this with about four touch points—depending on your group's strength, motivation, and clothing (again, be careful about girls wearing dresses). You'll want to go at least a third round. If the number of touch points proves solvable within a few minutes, give them another challenge.

After they've achieved something that appeared to be quite difficult for them, congratulate them on their amazing feat, and have them cheer for themselves.

Then ask these questions:

• **On a scale of one to 10, how difficult was this task?**

• **What made it difficult?**

• **What would have made it easier?**

• **How do you feel, in general about difficult tasks?**

GETTING THE POINT

On the Edge

Begin this section by having the kids actively respond to a series of which-would-be-more-difficult questions. Read the statements below. As you mention the first item, point to one wall in your room. As you mention the second item, point to the opposing wall. Have students move to the appropriate wall to indicate their response.

You'll need—
• *blank paper*
• *a pen or pencil for about every four students*

Would it be more difficult for you to give a 10-minute speech on a subject you know nothing about or make a fancy dinner for some important people?

Would it be more difficult for you to run a marathon or camp by yourself in the woods for three days?

Would it be more difficult for you to put your hand in a bucket of spiders or drink a big glass of raw eggs?

Would it be more difficult for you to walk through a mall in your underwear or sing the national anthem at a major league baseball game?

Would it be more difficult for you to tell a friend about Jesus or tell someone you don't know about Jesus?

Would it be more difficult for you to pray out loud in front of 200 people or give a five-minute sermon in front of your youth group?

Would it be more difficult for you to defend creation in your science class or defend a loner kid that nobody likes when he's picked on at lunch?

Would it be more difficult for you to tell the truth when you know you'll get in trouble for it or help your little brother with his homework when your friend wants to talk on the phone?

Would it be more difficult for you to give an offering regularly to your church or give two hours a week to work with the little kids at church?

Would it be more difficult for you to actually pay attention and listen to a whole sermon or sing worship songs with a full voice—no holding back?

As your kids are returning to their seats, ask them move their chairs into groups of four (three to five is okay). Have one person from each group come to you and get a blank piece of paper and a pen or pencil.

Have each group come up with a list of difficult things about being a Christian. What are some of the things that God wants them to do that aren't easy to do? Give the groups about three or four minutes. Be sure to walk around and observe to be sure they understand the question.

When the groups are done, have kids share an item off their lists. Keep sharing until it seems you've exhausted most of what they have.

Then say something like this: **The Christian life all boils down to two commands: Love God and love others.** *(Matthew 22:37-39)* **But sometimes, in order to do those two things well, we have to step out of our comfort zones. We have to get uncomfortable. God occasionally asks us to do things that are difficult for us.**

Ask: **When we do difficult things for God, where does our strength come from?** *This is actually a bit of a trick question. Our strength can come from many places—from our own reserves, from others cheering us on, or from God. The only reliable and sure source of strength, however, is God.*

Then tell your group they're going to look at a story in the Bible they've probably never seen before, about a woman who did something radical for God.

Meet Hammerhead

It's time for another spontaneous melodrama. In case you're not 100 percent clear what that is (say, because you chose to do this lesson first), you recruit kids to act out the parts in these short dramas. They don't have to learn any lines or rehearse. They act out what you read, as you read it, and repeat any lines that you read for their character. You'll only need two characters for this melodrama, one girl and one guy. Make sure the two you pick will ham it up with their characters.

You'll need—
• one copy of *Meet Hammerhead* (page 65)
• Bibles

Now read the story (**Meet Hammerhead** on page 65), pausing for the characters to act out the parts and say their lines.

After the melodrama is finished, thank your actors and have all your students turn in their Bibles to Judges 4:17-22 and read the biblical version of the story.

Then ask these questions:

• **Could you have done what Jael did? Why or why not?**

• **Why do you think she did it?**

• **Is this story teaching us that we should go out and put tent pegs through bad peoples' heads?** *Of course not. But it's easy for junior highers to get distracted by this and miss the point of the lesson. Don't spend too much time here and get sidetracked, but you will want to quickly explain to your kids that during Old Testament times people were judged by God according to the law of God. After Jesus came, judgment is connected to our trust in Jesus and God's grace. Wow! You* *may want to engage your students in a scintillating discussion of dispensationalism and substitutionary atonement. Or you could just move on.*

- **Is the Christian life easy or hard?** [This, again, is somewhat of a trick question. The Christian life is both. Jesus says his yoke is easy and his burden is light. The basic message of following Christ is fairly simple. But there are, without a doubt, tons of aspects of this life of discipleship that are difficult. Set your kids up. If they answer that it's hard, then ask if anyone thinks it's easy. See if you can get a little discussion and disagreement going. Then spring the both idea on them.]

- **What are some of the benefits of doing difficult things for God?** [It stretches our faith and makes us stronger and more prepared for future difficult situations. It causes us to trust in God to give us strength. It provides a reality check in our spiritual walk—are we committed to giving up everything for Jesus? And it can give us great joy when we see the results of our obedience.]

Step Up to the Plate

Pass out copies of **Step Up to the Plate** (page 66) and a pen or pencil to each of your sweet, lovely young teens (and to the rest of them, too). Direct

their attention, first, to the area at the top of the sheet that asks them to write down four difficult acts that God might want them to do. Brainstorm with your kids a bit, drawing from your earlier activities. Consider witnessing, relationship restoration, being nice to lonely people or jerks, loving family members, and obeying parents. Ask your students to write four areas meaningful to them.

Ask your students to

arrange the four acts they've chosen on the baseball diamond in order of the perceived difficulty (don't explain it this way, of course, unless your desired outcome is a bunch of blank stares. Well, on second thought, a bunch of blank stares is reality in junior high ministry much of the time!)

Instead, say something like this: **Write your four difficult acts on the baseball diamond with the least difficult on first base and the most difficult on home plate.**

Give your students a couple of minutes to complete this task.

Then move on to the final step. Ask your kids to pray silently for a minute, asking God which of these four things he might want them to try this week. After prayer, have your kids circle one of the bases to indicate the one they'll try this week. If you have time, ask a few willing students to share their answers. Before you close, remind them that God will be their source of strength and power in these situations if they rely on him.

MEET HAMMERHEAD

Characters
- Jael (a female)
- Sisera (a male)

Jael (pronounced jay-el) was kicking back in her tent one day, just a stone's throw away from a vicious battle. The enemies were getting thrashed by Jael's people—the Israelites. Jael said to herself, "I'm pretty sure I'm far enough from the battle to avoid any surprise problems."

No sooner had she said those words than Sisera shows up. He dives head first into Jael's tent, landing on the ground next to her. She gasps loudly. Then she starts pounding on him with her tiny clenched fists. Sisera roles out of the way and gasping, says, "You've gotta help me!"

Suddenly, Jael looks up with a facial expression that says, "Wow! I realize who this guy is!" Because at that moment, Jael realizes that Sisera is the top commander of the enemy army. She looks at him with fear. Then she starts to giggle. Then she breaks into uncontrollable laughter because she's got a plan. She mumbles to herself, "I've got a plan."

Jael takes on a sweet tone of voice and calmly says to Sisera, "Why don't you hide here in my tent?"

Sisera responds, "Okay."

Jael continues, "Let me get you something to drink."

Sisera says, "Okay."

Jael whips up a batch of her specialty: warm milk. Sisera slurps it down, still laying on the tent floor.

Then Jael starts to sing Sisera a lullaby. She sings so sweetly, and Sisera smiles a big goofy grin. Pretty soon Sisera falls asleep and begins to snore loudly.

Jael realizes that her plan has worked and lets out another huge laugh. Sisera snorts a bit and tosses around but doesn't wake up.

Jael walks to the corner of her tent, opens her tool box, and pulls out a hammer. Then she pulls one of the tent stakes out of the ground. It's stuck so she pulls and pulls, grunting the whole time. After continuing to grunt and pull, the tent stake finally comes flying out, sending Jael falling backward, right on top of Sisera. But this doesn't wake him either.

Jael creeps up to Sisera, places the tent stake against his temple, and, with three loud yells and swings of the hammer, drives the tent stake right through his head into the ground. Sisera convulses a few times, then lies still, dead.

Jael groans, "Yuck!" Then she does a little victory dance around Sisera.

The End

STEP UP TO THE PLATE

First pitch
Write four difficult acts that God might want you to do. Think of relationships, people that God would like you to reach out to, obedience to your parents, witnessing, and stuff like that.

1.

2.

3.

4.

Second pitch
Place the above four acts onto the baseball diamond below, ranked from least difficult to most difficult (least difficult at first base, most difficult at home plate):

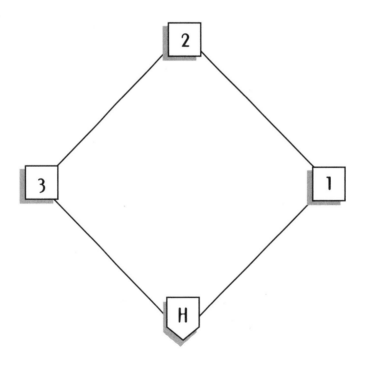

Third pitch
Pray and then circle one you'll try this week.

Bad Luck Boils

Job, on when life is unfair

Bible passage: Job 38:1-41

GOALS

Students will—

- *Consider the unfairness of life.*
- *Gain perspective on hardship from God's point of view.*
- *Write prayers to God, expressing their feelings about hardship.*

JUMP START

That's Not Fair!

Y ou'll begin this session with a game. It will be a set-up though. The idea is to create a lopsided scenario, with one team having all the advantages and the other team having none until some of your kids start shouting, "That's not fair!" If your group is anything like the average junior high group, this should take about three or four nanoseconds.

Divide your group into two teams. If you've got two grades, consider using seventh grade against eighth grade. You could also go girls against guys. If you choose the latter, stack the deck so the girls win (there are enough opportunities for guys to win out over girls in our world). Tell them they're going to play a game that is three rounds long. The team with the most points wins.

The first round is a simple game of Emotion Charades. If your kids don't know how to play charades, quickly explain the rules:

- **One person from the first team comes up and gets the emotion name from you. She has to act out this emotion for her team.**

> **You'll need—**
> - *no materials (although some sort of small candy prize for the winning team—half of your group—would add to the experience)*

- **Students cannot use any words or sounds at all and cannot spell the word with their hands or bodies.**
- **Teams shout out answers until the correct one is given.**
- **Give a time limit of 10 seconds. No points are awarded unless the team correctly guesses the answer within this time limit.**
- **An actor from the second team takes his turn.**
- **Play continues until each team has acted out its designated three words.**

Now you'll notice the answers for one team (Lightning Bolts) are fairly easy and the answers for the other team (Hailstones) are fairly difficult. You can let the kids create their own team names if you like. (The team names used here are based on Job 38.) Some of the players are bound to start complaining right away. Brush them off. Don't let them know the game is rigged. It will get more obvious in the second and third rounds of this game!

Lightning Bolts	Hailstones
1. Mad	1. Frustrated
2. Happy	2. Confused
3. Bored	3. Lonely

Award 1,000 points to the winning team. Hopefully, this will be the Lightning Bolts. But it won't matter if the Hailstones won this first round.

W hen you're reading through the Bible and get to Job, you can tell immediately that this book is—well, just so different. Maybe one reason is that, while the Bible tends to dictate or at least suggest answers, the book of Job specializes in questions. The man Job asks most of them: Since when does God reward righteousness with problems and trouble? Or if God's not in control here, who or what is? Isn't God the giver of good things? Then why tragedy after tragedy? Just what is God doing, anyway? So after Job, in the middle of his misery and loss, asks all of his questions, and after his friends sagely stroke their chins and give Clear Answers—at this point God blows into the scene, blows away all attempts at answers, and proceeds to ask four solid chapters of questions of his own. Job took the presence of God as the best available answer, and was satisfied.

They won't win any more!

Round two is the Famous Couples Match Game. You'll need three competitors from each team to stand together representing their peers. You'll address the Lightning Bolts and say the name of someone famous who has a famous partner. The team representatives have five seconds to come up with one answer. (They cannot offer lots of answers until they guess correctly.) After the Lightning Bolts have had a chance, address the Hailstones with the next pair. Continue alternating until each team has had four questions. Keep the game moving quickly, ignoring any complaints that it isn't fair. The team with the most correct answers gets 1,000 points.

Lightning Bolts' Clues

- Bill Clinton [the answer is Hillary]
- Homer Simpson [the answer is Marge]
- Joseph, the father of Jesus [the answer is Mary]
- Adam [the answer is Eve]

Hailstones' Clues

- Lucille Ball [the answer is Desi Arnez]
- John F. Kennedy [the answer is Jackie Onassis]
- Moses [the answer is Zipporah]
- Maria from *The Sound of Music* [the answer is Georg (pronounced Gay-org) Van Trapp]

The Lightning Bolts probably have won both rounds. So make the last round worth 5,000 points so the Hailstones can still have the hope of winning. The final challenge is a quick test of geography knowledge. Have teams present four new contestants each, if possible, to represent them. Tell them you'll ask a question about geography, and the team reps will need to come up with one answer. There's no real time limit on this one—they only need to offer an answer within a reasonable time frame.

Lightning Bolts

1. Name a country in North America other than the United States. [Canada or Mexico]
2. Name the range of mountains that runs through Colorado. [the Rockies]
3. Name a state that begins with the letter A. [Alaska, Arkansas, Alabama, Arizona]
4. What do the letters D and C stand for in Washington, D.C.? [District of Columbia]
5. Name a country in western Europe. [Austria, Belgium, Denmark, Finland, France, Germany, Greece, Ireland, Italy, Liechtenstein, Luxembourg, Netherlands, Norway, Portugal, Spain, Sweden, Switzerland, United Kingdom]

Hailstones

1. Name the official language spoken in the African country of Rwanda. [French]
2. Name the ocean off the east coast of Africa. [Indian Ocean]
3. Name the country that lies directly south of Detroit, Michigan. [Canada]
4. Name the chain of islands that stretches off the southwestern edge of Alaska. [the Aleutians]
5. To know the capital of India, what would you need to know? [the controlling political party, who determines where the capital is]

Okay, by now you've had kids from the Hailstones ranting and raving. The kid with a lawyer dad has probably already had his father draft a lawsuit against you. Several are threatening in that wonderful junior high way. "This game is stupid—I'm not gonna play" and "Man, why don't you just give the other team the answers—we're just gonna sit here."

If you brought some kind of prize for the winning team, such as small candies, award them now.

Even if the Hailstones were somehow able to pull off a win (anything's possible in junior high ministry), they'll still feel like their questions were unfairly difficult.

So in a sympathetic voice, say: It did seem like some of those questions for the Hailstones were a bit hard, didn't it?

Then ask these questions:
- **Did that game seem fair?**
- **What about those of you who won—did it seem fair to you?**
- **Does life ever feel like that—totally unfair?**
- **Can you share a story about a situation that was unfair?**

Hey, teacher of junior highers! I've worked with young teens long enough to learn a couple things about people who teach them: They are some of the most important, underappreciated people in the church! That's right. You are extremely important to God's kingdom.

Most of the people in the church probably think you're a little off-balance to work with junior highers. This often comes from a misunderstanding about these awesome kids. Many people view the inescapable squirreliness of junior highers as a truly bad thing to be waited out—endured—until they are capable of adult behavior (whatever that means).

But here's the truth: the transition junior highers are in the middle of—the restlessness, the short attention spans, the emotional swings—is all part of the change in their lives being orchestrated by God! Our sovereign designer *made young teens the way they are!* Nothing God makes is bad.

Enjoy your group's unique junior highness. See them as God's special creations—exactly the way he wanted them to be at this point in their lives.

GETTING THE POINT

Life's Not Fair!

Hey, Wait a Minute! (page 72) uses three sections to gradually teach the idea that life is full of unfairness. The first section is three case studies on unfairness that junior highers can relate to. The second section gives your kids an opportunity to assess degrees of unfairness and sets up thinking and discussion on different events. And the final section asks them to reflect on

unfairness in their own lives.

Guide your students through the sheet one section at a time. Give them a few minutes to complete a section on their own (or do it together orally), then discuss the section before moving on to the next one.

It All Depends on Your Perspective

Ask your students if they know what *perspective* is. Some will think they do. A few may. Even if someone can come up with a good definition, most of your students will probably be a little fuzzy on this concept. So help them understand with the following little demonstration.

Ask a volunteer to stand in the middle of your room, about four feet in front of you, facing the front of the room. Now ask two other volunteers to help "limit the first volunteer's perspective." Give the second and third volunteers each a poster board or large piece of paper and ask the kids to hold them on either side of the first volunteer's head, with most of the poster board out in front of the person. This creates a narrow tunnel for the person to see from and her peripheral vision is completely gone. She should only be able to see what's directly in front of her.

Ask for three more volunteers. Explain a brief sketch for them to pantomime in a way the student without perspective cannot hear. One of these volunteers should walk across the front of the room, from one side to the other, pretending to paddle a canoe. This is all the watching volunteer should be able to see. When the paddler is out of the view of the observer, the other two pantomime trying to dump the canoe, and the person in the canoe acts out tipping but not flipping over. The actors should be completely silent.

Have them perform their sketch. After they're finished, ask the observer to describe what she saw. Her answer will be something like this: "Someone was canoeing across the front of the room."

Remove the poster boards and have the actors perform the sketch again exactly as they did it the first time. Now have the observer explain what she saw that she missed the first time. Have her explain why she could see more the second time.

After thanking everyone for helping, explain that the observer had a limited perspective the first time. Only the second time, with a complete perspective, was she able to see the whole story.

Explain to your students: The same is true in our lives all the time. God, who has an eternal perspective, can see everything. When things happen that seem unfair to us, God sees it from a different perspective than us. He understands what we don't understand.

Have your students imagine living a long, long time ago—say 2,000 years before Christ. Ask them to describe a person who would have "had it all" by the standards of the time. Give them categories to consider if they need help: What kinds of animals would you have? How many of each? How much land might you have? How about family?

Ask for six volunteers to come up front. Assign the following roles: Job, Job's sheep, Job's cow, Job's camel, Job's field, Job's kid.

Tell the story of Job this way:

Job was a happy man. Show us a big smile, Job. He had lots of sheep *(ask the sheep to wave)*, lots of cows *(ask the cow to wave)*, lots of camels *(ask the camel to wave)*, lots of land *(ask the land to wave)*, and some swell kids *(ask the kid to wave)*. He had it all *(ask Job to smile again)*. But Job had a bad day. Show us a big frown, Job. All his sheep died *(the sheep should die)*, his cows died *(the cow should die)*, his camels died *(the camel should die)*, his land burned *(have the land croak, too)*, and his kids died *(the kid should die)*. Show us another big frown, Job. Job's friends tried to convince him that it was his own fault. Job's wife tried to get him to curse

God and die. But Job knew God must have allowed all this bad stuff for a reason. Eventually Job started demanding that God tell him the reason.

Thank your actors, and have them sit down. Then have everyone turn in their Bibles to Job 38:1-41. Tell your students that this is only one small part of God's answer. Read the passage to your students while they follow along.

Before the meeting, make sure you read the Job chapter a few times so you are able to read it with flair. Where God uses sarcasm, you add a sarcastic tone of voice. Speak strongly when God speaks strongly.

When you're done reading, ask:

- **What was God trying to say to Job? Why did God ask him all those questions?**
- **What was different about God's perspective?**
- **How would you have responded if you were Job?**
- **What can we learn about how we should respond when life isn't fair?**

Here's What I Think, God

Tell your students that you're going to ask them to do a little writing.

Say: There are lots of ways to pray. One great way to pray is to write your prayers to God on paper—it makes you think about your

You'll need—
- *copies of Here's What I Think, God (page XX)*
- *pens or pencils*

words. That's what we're going to do now. I'm going to pass out a piece of paper, and I want you to write a prayer to God about unfairness in life. If you have anything in your life right now that's unfair, write to God about it. If you don't have anything unfair going on right now, write God your feelings about unfairness in life and what you've learned in this time together.

Now distribute copies of **Here's What I Think, God** (page 73). Your kids should still have their pens or pencils. Give them about five minutes to write their prayers. Then ask if some will read their prayers out loud while everyone else prays along silently.

Hey, Wait a Minute!

Three Little Stories

Hi, I'm Tim and my life rots! My parents divorced a year ago and they hate each other. They constantly try to use me to get back at each other. Is this fair? ❑ Yes   ❑ No

Hey, Tina here. My best friend Paige stole my boyfriend last week. When I confronted her about it, she said, "I liked him better than I liked you." Is this fair? ❑ Yes   ❑ No

I'm Tommy, and I'm toast! I saved all my money for an entire year to buy a new mountain bike. I ordered, and paid for, the bike I wanted from a store down the street, and the store went out of business before my bike came in. Is this fair? ❑ Yes   ❑ No

How Unfair Is This?

Rate the following based on how unfair each is by placing an X along each line.

Super Fair   Mega Unfair

1. The teacher gives you a lower grade because she doesn't like you.
2. Someone starts a false rumor about you.
3. Your parents are less strict with your younger brother.
4. You get sick and miss the most important game of the season.
5. Some other kid gets the solo in the musical because she knows the choir director.
6. A tornado destroys your home.
7. You slip on some ice and break your leg—the doc says you'll be in a cast for three months.
8. For a science project, your assigned partner won't do his part of the work.
9. Your friend got paid a dollar more per hour for baby-sitting a certain family.
10. Your parents decide to move to another town right in the middle of your school year.

My Unfair Life

1. What's something unfair—something on a big scale—that you've experienced in your life?

2. What's something kind of unfair that's happened to you in the last week or two?

3. How have you reacted to these situations?

HERE'S WHAT I THINK, GOD

Write a prayer to God about an unfairness in your life right now or tell him your feelings about life's unfairness and what you've learned in this lesson.

Dear God,

In Jesus' name, amen!

Sam the Mighty Man

Samson, on making choices based on values rather than on experience

Bible passage: Judges 16:4-21

GOALS

Students will—

- *Discuss different ways people make choices.*
- *Understand what it means to make values-based decisions.*
- *List values and apply them to one decision they have to make.*

JUMP START

Let's Make a Choice

You'll start this session with a version of the old game show "Let's Make a Deal." Gather the bags or boxes you prepared (see the "You'll need—" box at left). When your group time begins, let everyone know they're going to play a game show.

You'll need—
- *about six boxes or bags, each containing one prize. Most prizes should be "good" things (small bag of Skittles or M&Ms or other candy, a quarter or a dollar, etc.), though maybe a third of the prizes should be "bad" things (can of dog food, dirty sock, etc.). The more time you want to take for this part of the lesson, the more bags you'll need (up to 10). (Now don't whine about this little preparation to make this activity work well... these lessons have required so little preparation up to now. You can do just a little bit of prep for one lesson, can't you?)*
- *a roll of dimes*

Switch into your best game-show-host voice and announce: **It's time to play, "Let's Make a Choice!" The game where contestants are asked to make a choice and then live with it!**

Here's how the game works. You'll ask for a contestant to volunteer (if no one volunteers, pick someone—c'mon, be ruthless, you're the teacher!). When the volunteer comes forward, ask him in your schmaltzy game-show-host voice to choose one of the bags or boxes. Don't let him see in the bag, just have him choose one. Now try to talk him out of that bag. Offer him a dime to pass up the bag. If he says yes, give him the dime and have him sit down. If he says no, offer him two dimes.

Have fun with this. You'll have several contestants, and ideally, you'd like to get some of them to opt out of opening their selected bags. Have some of them open their bags. Once students have opened a bag, have them take their item and sit down. If they get something good, you might consider an offer to trade their item for the unknown contents of a different bag. You'll have to do your best tempting here! Continue with contestants until all your items are gone or until you've used up so much of your lesson time that you'll have to condense the next three sections into 30 seconds.

After the game is over, ask these questions:
- **Was it difficult to make choices? Why or why not?**
- **How did you feel when your choice brought a bad result?**
- **How did you feel when your choice brought a good result?**

John Grisham's fictitious Firm wasn't the first to engineer a one-night stand in order to control a man, whether it meant keeping him quiet or squeezing information out of him. With Samson it was the latter. Singlehandedly, the strongman had stormed through Philistine cities and fields, leaving a bloody wake behind him. Because even the Philistines could see that it was usually a woman who, in some way or another, inflamed him into action, they bribed his new wife to wheedle out of him the information they needed to end the destruction. As usual, Samson responded with his hormones before he consulted his principles—or even his memory.

GETTING THE POINT

How Do Ya Choose?

*C*ontinue *your line of questioning:*

• **What are different ways that people make decisions? In other words, how do people decide which choice to choose?** [We all use different criteria when making decisions. Some questions we ask ourselves: What's best for me? What would please me the most at this moment? What's the best choice in the long run? What choice would please God?]

You'll need
• *no materials*

Read the following three case studies. After each, pause and discuss the way the main character made his or her decision.

Flip

My name is Philip—but my friends call me Flip. The other day a bunch of my friends decided to skip school and hang out by a pond near our school. They bugged me and bugged me to come with them. I wanted to go and was pretty convinced I wouldn't get caught because my parents were out of town and my older sister was taking care of me. But I decided not to go because we were going to be learning some stuff in my science class that day that I thought would be important for my goal to be a doctor some day.

Meg

My name's Meg, and I'm in eighth grade. Last year I had to make the toughest decision of my life: my divorced parents asked me to decide which one of them I would live with. I love them both—so it was hard. In the end I chose to live with my dad because he's got way more money than my mom and I thought I'd have a better life there. I still see my mom all the time, anyhow.

Tina

Hi, I'm Tina, and my recent decision wasn't that big of a deal. I only had $20 to spend and had to make a choice whether I would buy a cool shirt that was on sale or a great CD I've been wanting. I went with the shirt since it was on sale and I could get the CD some other time.

Say: **We all make decisions constantly. Some decisions are big ones like Meg's. Some are no big deal like Tina's. Many people make decisions based on what's best for them at that moment. But those are often some of the worst decisions. Good decisions are made based on your long-term values. And the best decisions of all are based on God's values. If your values are God's values and you make decisions based on them, then you will be a great decision-maker.**

Ask:

• **What's a value?** [Something you believe that affects the way you live.]

• **Give me some examples of values.** [Depending on your group, this may be a difficult question until they hear one or two answers. If no one offers an answer, suggest a couple of your own.]

Now tell your students you're going to name a value and you want them to come up with a scenario and then describe how the value would impact the decision.

Read this list, pausing between each one for responses:

1. **I think it's important to treat other people with respect.**

2. **I think listening is more important than talking.**

3. **I want to please God with every decision I make.**

4. **I want to be a virgin when I get married.**

5. **I value good health.**

Kung Fu Bible Theater

You've seen those martial arts movies where the English has been dubbed over the original language, and the words don't quite match the movement of the actors' mouths. In fact, the spoken lines of the characters can seem downright silly. Translation's a messy job! Well, today you'll tell your group the story of Samson and Delilah—like a foreign Kung Fu movie with English voices dubbed in.

The difference between this activity being kind of goofy or downright hilarious all boils down to one thing: the quality of the narration. If you're a bit of a ham yourself, go for it! Otherwise, recruit someone beforehand to be the narrator.

You'll need—
- Bibles
- 5 copies of *Kung Fu Bible Theater* (page 79)
- optional: a CD or tape soundtrack from Enter the Dragon *or some other martial arts movie (and don't forget the equipment to play it)*

You begin the whole thing by announcing, with a grand voice: It's time for...Kung Fu Bible Theater!

After the drama (Shakespeare and Bruce Lee would both turn in their graves), ask if students know about Samson. Ask if they know some of the amazing feats of strength he did. If they don't, show them these verses:

- **Samson rips apart a lion with his bare hands (Judges 14:5-6).**
- **Samson catches 300 foxes (Judges 15:4-5).**
- **Samson kills 1,000 guys with a donkey jawbone (Judges 15:14-15).**
- **Samson carries some big ol' city gates a long way (Judges 16:3).**
- **Samson pushes down the temple with his bare hands (Judges 16:29-30).**

Then ask your students to turn in their Bibles to Judges 16:4-21, and read the real account of Samson and Delilah.

After you finish reading, ask:
- **Why did Samson tell Delilah the secret of his strength?**
- **What values of Samson's did he forget about when he made the decision to tell her?**

Students *may* be able to pull off this Kung Fu Bible Theater (see above) if they're confident and have a little rehearsal time. Whoever narrates will greatly benefit from reading over the script a couple times. But the most important quality of a good Kung Fu Bible Theater narrator is the ability to watch the acting unfold and make the dialogue and sound effects match up.

Here's how it works. It's somewhat like a regular drama, but the characters make no sounds and speak no lines. They only act the parts and move their mouths for the lines. The characters need to see the narration before performing to know the basic story line. Then when you're ready for this part of the lesson, they act out the play. The narrator should be offstage. This is best accomplished from the back of the room with a microphone. But if your group is smaller and you don't have a sound system, the narrator can stand off to the side and speak loudly.

If you didn't get the story line to the kids ahead of time, just give each of them a copy of **Kung Fu Bible Theater** (page 79) and have them wing it!

My Values, My Decisions

It's time for a little application. Remind your kids that they all make decision every day—some almost unnoticeable and some important.

Distribute copies of **My Values, My Decisions** (page 81) to each student, along with a pen or pencil. **My Values, My Decisions** asks them to reflect on a decision they need to make. Give them a minute to try to think of something.

> ### *You'll need—*
> • *copies of My Values, My Decisions (page 81)*
> • *pens or pencils*

For some this will be simple; others may not come up with anything. If you have students who, after a minute or two, cannot think of a decision they need to make, ask them to think of a decision they may need to make in the next month or so. Either way, your students should write this decision on the first line of the sheet.

The second section asks them to list any values they have that might affect their decisions. If you have a small group, circulate among your kids and help them with this. If your group is larger, break into small groups with supervising adults to help in each group. But if it's you with 30 kids (you are to be both pitied and revered), you can still expect them to do this.

Finally, ask them to make a decision based on their long-term values. Suggest that it would be best if their long-term values matched up with God's values! Ask a few students to share their problems, values, and decisions. If you have broken into small groups, have several students share in each group.

Close your time in prayer, asking God to give everyone his wisdom to make good decisions, and the patience to choose the long-range over the immediate.

Kung Fu Bible Theater

Cast
- Narrator (speaks *all* the lines, though in the voices of Samson and Delilah)
- Samson (acts only, adds sound effects when called for)
- Delilah (acts only, adds sound effects when called for)
- Philistines (two or three will do —act only, with sound effects)

IN SAMSON'S VOICE: *(to the audience)* My name is Samson, and I'm a prophet of God. I made a commitment to him that I'll never cut my hair—it's kind of a sign that I'm living for him. So God's given me great strength. And I know I'll loose it if I ever cut my hair.

IN DELILAH'S VOICE: *(to the audience)* I'm Delilah. I like Samson, but I like money more. And the Philistines have offered me a bunch of money to find out how Samson can loose his strength. *(turning to Samson)* Oh Samson, you are so big and strong. I've always wondered how you could be so strong. Won't you tell me the secret of your strength?

IN SAMSON'S VOICE: Well...uhh... hmm... uhhh...sure, honey, I'll tell you. If you lace up my shoes the wrong way, I'll become a 90-pound weakling.

IN DELILAH'S VOICE: Oh, I see. Why don't you take a nap? *(Samson lies down and sleeps. Delilah pretends to mess with his shoelaces. Delilah talks to herself.)* I'll mess with his shoelaces and tie them the wrong way. *(giggles)* Okay, come on in Philistines.

(The Philistines enter and have a martial arts-style fight with Samson. The narrator adds grunting, punching, screaming, and smacking sound effects. The Philistines, being beaten, flee the stage.)

IN DELILAH'S VOICE: *(pouting)* Samson! You didn't tell me the truth! How can I be your girlfriend if you won't tell me the truth? How can you loose your strength?

IN SAMSON'S VOICE: Well...uhh... hmm... uhhh...okay, I'll tell you. If you mess up my hair—I mean mess it up, I'll loose all my strength.

IN DELILAH'S VOICE: Why don't you take another nap, honey. *(Samson lies down and sleeps again. Delilah messes up his hair, talking to herself.)* I'll mess up his hair. Then he'll be weak and I'll get my money. Oh, Philistines!

(Again, Samson and the Philistines engage in a martial arts fight complete with sound effects, and once again flee the stage area.)

IN DELILAH'S VOICE: *(whiny)* Sam. How can you say you care about me when you keep lying to me. Tell me the truth!

IN SAMSON'S VOICE: Well...uhh... hmm... uhhh...okay, I'll tell you. If you tickle me while I'm sleeping I'll become just like any other man.

IN DELILAH'S VOICE: Why don't you take another nap, honey. *(Samson lies down and sleeps again. Delilah tickles him and speaks to herself.)* I'll tickle him a little, then call in the Philistines and collect my cash! Oh, Philistines!

(For the third time, Samson and the Philistines engage in a short martial arts fight with sound effects by the narrator. For the third time, the Philistines flee the stage.)

IN DELILAH'S VOICE: *(crying)* I'm about to give up on this relationship! You say you care about me—but it's just lies, lies, lies. This can't go on! If you don't tell me the truth, you'll loose me.

IN SAMSON'S VOICE: Well...uhh... hmm... uhhh...okay, I'll tell you. And I'll tell you the truth this time. I've been set apart for God since birth, and as a symbol, I've never had my hair cut. If someone cut my hair, I'd be an average guy—no more super-strength.

IN DELILAH'S VOICE: Why don't you take another nap, honey. *(Samson lies down and sleeps again. Delilah pretends to cut his hair while talking to herself)* Cut, cut, cut. It's that simple, huh? I'll cut it all off, and then call the Philistines. Oh, Philistines!

(This time, as the martial arts fight between Samson and the Philistines unfolds, Samson has no strength and can't fight well at all. The Philistines quickly overcome him and hold him, eventually taking him away.)

IN SAMSON'S VOICE: *(being led off-stage, addressing the audience)* Don't do what I did. I let my short-term desires override my long-term goals. I made decisions without thinking about my values!

The End

My Values, My Decisions

Write a decision you need to make.

What are a few values you have that might influence this decision?

1.

2.

3.

4.

5.

Based on your long-term values, what would be the best decision for you to make?

Gidddy the Frightened Wimp

Gideon, on how God sees us

Bible passage: Judges 6:11-18

GOALS

Students will—

- *Describe themselves.*
- *Describe themselves through God's eyes.*
- *Write letters to God, telling him what difference this makes.*

JUMP START

Who Am I?

Begin your time by passing out blank paper and pens or pencils to each junior higher. Ask them to write answers to the following questions and to not let anyone see their answers.

- **My favorite color is...**
- **My favorite pizza topping is...**
- **My least favorite class in school is...**
- **My favorite musician or musical group is...**
- **My favorite TV show is...**

Ask your kids to write their names at the top of the papers, then collect them all. Quickly glance through the papers and select seven or eight that are readable and represent a wide cross-section of the kids in your group (maybe you only have seven or eight kids—then this would be everyone).

Tell them the goal is to see if they can guess who the different people are merely by the description you'll read from the answers. If your group has eight or less students have them play independently. If you have between nine and 40 students, have them work in teams of three to five.

(If your group has more than 40 students, consider a variation: Use a group of your adult leaders—have them jot down the answers to the questions and let the kids guess who's who of the leaders. Or you could select about 10 students to stand up front and quickly fill out the sheets. Then have the groups guess who's who while the student representatives stay up front. Seeing the participants will make this feasible even if the other kids don't know them.)

Read the five answers on one sheet and ask the students or groups to shout out their guess.

Then say: Will the real person who has these answers please stand up?

Repeat the process as many times as necessary.

You'll need—
- blank paper
- pencils or pens

GETTING THE POINT

Who Am I, Really?

Distribute copies of **Who Am I, Really?** (page 86). If you didn't have all your students answer the questions for the opening game, you'll have to pass out pens or pencils now. Ask them to fill out the sheet, drawing a picture of them-

You'll need—
- copies of *Who Am I, Really?* (page 86)

God seems nothing less than infatuated with doing the most with the least. It actually seems to delight him to take a deceitful Jacob and turn him into Israel's namesake. Or to use the whore Rahab to save a pair of Hebrew spies from capture—and possibly the entire Israeli army from defeat. Or—in Gideon's case—to use the youngest son in the weakest clan of a divided tribe to galvanize Israel for revolt against an army of occupation. And to leave no doubt in Gideon's mind about just how low God will stoop to prove this point, God patiently waited out Gideon's second-guessing, his doubt, his fearfulness. Then, finally convinced that he was actually able to do what God had said all along he could do, Gideon got up and did it.

selves, then answering the questions about who they are. This will be easy and fun for a few kids, but it will be somewhere between a little difficult and downright tortuous for most kids.

This exercise forces them to reflect on themselves, and this is something few junior highers want to do. They're going through the most radical transition of their lives—from childhood to adulthood—and to say the change is tough is like saying climbing the outside of the World Trade Center using only your fingertips is difficult. But the whole point of this lesson is to juxtapose their flawed view of themselves against God's view of who they are and who they can be.

When they've finished (this should take about five to seven minutes), ask them to share their sheets with one other person. This won't be too difficult for kids with good friends in your group. But it's fairly vulnerable sharing for students who don't feel like they know anyone in your group well. Be sensitive to this. Give them a couple of minutes to do this.

Say something like this: **Most young teens don't think highly of themselves. We're usually a lot quicker to pick out all our faults than to name anything positive about ourselves. God sees you differently, though. He sees what you can become, with his help. And that's always awesome!**

Greetings, Big Dufus

Say: **There was a guy in the Bible who had a hard time seeing himself from God's perspective.**

Ask three students to come up to the front of the room to help you with a little reading exercise. Give each of them a copy of **Greetings, Big Dufus** (page 87) and keep one copy for yourself. They are to follow along as you read the story and every time you pause, they are to read their assigned lines. One should read all the statements numbered one, another should read all the statements numbered two, and somebody should read all the threes. Make sure the three volunteers understand their roles.

You'll need—
• *four copies of* ***Greetings, Big Dufus*** *(page 87)*
• *Bibles*

Tell your group that you're going to read a paraphrase of the story of Giddy. There will be a bunch of times where you'll stop in the middle of the sentence and the three volunteers will offer three possible ways to finish the sentence. The job of the audience is to vote on the correct answer.

Now read the story, pausing at the appropriate places for the readers to offer their possible answers. Then ask the rest of the group to vote on the correct answer before continuing. The correct answers are in bold. This doesn't have to be a competition—it's for the fun of it!

After you finish this reading, have your students turn in their Bibles to Judges 6:11-18 and read the real story.

Then ask:

• **How did Gideon view himself?** [As the weakest of the weak.]

• **What words would he have used to describe himself?**

• **How did God see Gideon?** [As a mighty warrior.]

• **Why did God see Gideon differently than Gideon saw himself?** [God sees from an eternal perspective; he sees who we can *become*, with his help. This is a tough question. The answer, however, is the key to this lesson—so see if you can steer the kids to discovering the answer themselves. So Gideon may have been right—he might have been the weakest of the weak. But with God, he was a mighty warrior.]

• **What can we learn about how God views us from Gideon's story?** [God sees each of us with tons of potential. If we rely on him, he will do great things through us.]

How God Sees Me

God sees our potential because he knows what we can be if we rely on him. In this final step, you'll try to help your students reflect on what that statement means for their own lives.

You'll need—
• copies of *How God Sees Me* (page 88)
• pens or pencils

Pass out copies of **How God Sees Me** (page 88). Your kids should still have pencils or pens from their earlier use. This page has two halves. The first half asks them to reflect on how God might see them. This is a conceptual stretch for the more concrete-thinking young adolescents. You'll have to walk alongside sixth graders, if you have them. And even some of your seventh grade boys may struggle with what this means. You want them to use their imaginations— to dream about what God might want to use them for, to imagine where in life God could be leading them, to wrestle with God's unquestioned love for them.

The second half of the page asks the kids to write a short letter to God expressing what difference this understanding of God's perspective could make in their lives.

It would be great, at the end of your time, if a few kids were willing to share their answers. This is fairly vulnerable sharing, however, so make sure you protect anyone who chooses to open up from any teasing or judging.

Close your session with group prayer. Have your kids express to God, in one to three words, what they're thankful for. Explain this to your kids, then start by saying, "God, I'm thankful for..." and then let kids finish the sentence. Finish the prayer time by thanking God yourself for seeing so much potential in each of us.

WHO AM I, REALLY?

Draw a picture of yourself.

Answer these questions about yourself:
- What three words would you use to describe yourself?

- What two things do you like about your personality?

- What one thing would you change about yourself, if you could?

GREETINGS, BIG DUFUS

adapted from Judges 6:11-18

Giddy had a little problem on his hands. He was afraid. After all—
   1. His family was being terrorized by a pack of bears.
   2. His people were at war.
   3. He was in danger of getting some very serious paper cuts.

So, while most of the men were out fighting in the war, our pal Giddy was—
   1. Hiding.
   2. Surfing.
   3. Spying.

He was afraid that the enemy would take his wheat, so he was busy threshing grain in a—
   1. Castle.
   2. Lion's den.
   3. Winepress.

An angel from God came to him and greeted him by saying—
   1. Greetings, Big Dufus.
   2. God is with you, Mighty Warrior.
   3. Don't run and hide, man.

Giddy answered back—
   1. How can God be with us when all this bad stuff is happening to us?
   2. Who are you and why are you bugging me while I'm hiding in this winepress?
   3. I'll go where God sends me and do what God asks.

God spoke to him and said—
   1. Stand up and be a man!
   2. Would you relax—I've got everything under control.
   3. Aren't I, God, sending you?

Giddy still responded—
   1. But I'm the weakest man in my family and my family is the weakest in the clan.
   2. I will trust you and go, God.
   3. Can't you send me to Taco Bell instead?

God spoke again and said—
   1. Oh, okay, I'll get someone else.
   2. Wow, why did I pick such a whiner?
   3. I'll be with you and you'll win the battle.

HOW GOD SEES ME

Some words that God might use to describe me (think *mighty warrior*)...

A way that God might want to use my life...

When God looks at me, he sees... *(check only one)*
- ❏ the answer below this one
- ❏ his child whom he loves
- ❏ the answer above this one

Write a letter to God, expressing to him what difference this understanding could make in your life. How might you act differently now that you know God thinks so highly of you?

Dear God,

All my love, your child, _____

Weather Man

Jesus, on his power in the middle of your problems

Bible passage: Mark 4:35-41

Students will—

GOALS

- *List problems of junior highers.*
- *Identify one or two problems of their own.*
- *Ask Jesus to help them in the middle of their problems.*

JUMP START

Houston, We Have a Problem!

Tell your students you're going to play a game that will require some daring volunteers. If your group is outgoing and full of kids who are willing to try anything, you won't need any prizes. But if your group is a bit more timid, you may want to have a bag of miniature candy bars or some other prize that you can use to bait contestants.

Explain that this game is a little like Truth or Dare except that there aren't any truth questions. Every round is a dare. Some of the dares will be no big deal. Anyone would do them. But some will ask you to do something that might be a little strange or goofy. Assure them that none of the dares will ask them to do something inappropriate (then you might want to snicker a bit to toss a little doubt in their minds!). Each contestant will draw a slip from the dare pile. After reading the dare aloud, they have two options: They can

You'll need—
- *one copy of **I Have a Problem with This!** (page 92), cut into squares*
- *optional bag of candy or some other prize for about 10 kids*

say, "No problem!" and complete the dare or they can say, "I have a problem with this!" and put the dare slip back in the pile and select another. If they choose to pass on the first dare, they must complete the second one they choose whether it's easier or harder than the first.

If you've decided to use candy prizes to bait contestants, explain that everyone who completes a dare will get a prize. Be sure you make it clear that there will be no option to back out if they volunteer.

Now ask for volunteers and have them, one at a time, come forward. It doesn't matter whether you use all the dare slips or not. Judge how long you keep the game going by the size of your group, the quantity of volunteers you get, and the amount of time you have. (To receive the mathematical equation for this computation, send a self-addressed, stamped envelope and $5 for postage and handling, to Youth Spec—or on second thought, just wing it. Besides, the publisher of this book would probably just buy donuts with the five bucks.)

After you've finished the game and had a good laugh, ask these questions:

- **Why were some of those a problem and others weren't any problem at all?**
- **What makes a situation in life a problem?** [Usually, a situation becomes a problem when the solution is unclear or difficult.]

More than one boat rowed out into the Sea of Tiberius before their sails caught the wind for an overnight trip to the other shore. Aboard one of the boats was the rabbi. It had been a draining week—answering the skepticism of the religious leaders, healing the maladies of the commoners, standing up to his own family who thought he had finally taken this messiah stuff too far and were ready to pack him off for his own good. He couldn't sit down to a meal without drawing a crowd. Exhaustion drove the rabbi to sleep before the boat was a thousand yards offshore. Even the squall, which descended out of nowhere and whipped up six-foot waves that threatened to capsize the boat, didn't waken him. It took more than a couple shoves from his followers to get him out of his bunk and aware of the peril. Once he surveyed the situation, though, he seemed to think there was more peril in their fear than in the weather.

GETTING THE POINT

Big Problem? No Problem!

Tape the sign that says BIG PROBLEM! on one wall of your room and the sign that says NO PROBLEM! on the opposite wall. Then read the following problems, asking your students to get up out of their seats and move to one wall or the other to register their opinions about the difficulty of each problem.

- **You received an F on a major test and don't know how to tell your parents.**
- **You're in a big-time fight with your best friend.**
- **You forgot to put on deodorant today and you stink!**
- You found out that your parents are considering a divorce.
- You can't remember your locker combination.
- Somehow, though you don't know how, you've ticked off the biggest bully in the school.
- You want the new CD of your favorite group, but you're two dollars short.
- You slept through your alarm on the day you have to give a speech in your first period class.
- You found out that the chicken you ate at lunch today is making everyone who ate it sick.
- You're starting to have some real questions and doubts about Christianity.
- You've got to decide whether to go to an amusement park with some kids you don't really know or roam around the mall with your best friend.
- Your uncle, who's not a Christian, asks you to explain all this "Jesus stuff" to him.
- You can't decide what to wear for your school picture.
- Your family can't afford for you to go to camp this year, and everyone else is going.

- You hurt your mom's feelings yesterday with a comment you made to her.
- You're growing faster than anyone you know, so kids are starting to make fun of you.
- You have a book report due tomorrow, and you can't find the book.

Acknowledge that everyone has problems—they're a normal part of life. But sometimes in junior high, problems can loom larger as freedoms begin to increase and teenage life sets in with adulthood just around the corner.

Write PROBLEMS OF JUNIOR HIGHERS at the top of your overhead transparency or butcher paper. Then ask kids to brainstorm for a few minutes, listing as many problems that they and their peers face as they can think of. Write them on the transparency or paper (or ask another adult present to be the scribe).

After you get a big list, ask: **What difference does it make that you're a Christian when you're faced with these problems?**

Lead a discussion around this question. Don't allow mindless answers like God makes them all go away. Push the kids for real answers. If someone has the guts to say, "I'm not sure it makes any difference," don't bash him for his answer. Instead, encourage the kids that an honest approach to this process is the best way to get a handle on it.

Ask: **Does God, in the Bible, ever promise that he'll take away all your problems?** [No. But this is a common misconception of young teen Christians—and sometimes older Christians.]

What *does* the Bible promise us about problems? [Primarily, the Bible promises we can count on having problems and God will be with us in the midst of them. The Bible also promises the Holy Spirit will comfort us and give us wisdom and guidance if we ask for it. Your kids may or may not have an answer for this, and that's okay. The answer will be cleared up as you move through the next section.]

FLASHBACK

The Weather Man

Distribute copies of **The Weather Man** (page 93) and pens or pencils to each student. If your kids didn't bring Bibles, guilt them and shame them. No, seriously, if they don't have Bibles, pass a few out. Ask them to get in groups of two or three and work through the questions together. Each group should have at least one Bible. Give them about five to eight minutes to complete this.

After they've had enough time to complete the questions, pull their attention back to the front and review the correct answers (which are purposefully easy—it's good to let your kids succeed!).

Here are the correct answers:

1. Jesus
2. The disciples
3. A big storm started and the waves got huge
4. They might die
5. Sleeping in the back of the boat
6. "Be still"
7. He was with them

Point out the obvious. Jesus was with the disciples in the midst of this huge problem. And he does the same for us every day. He might not always step in and stop the problem like he did for the disciples. But he will always be with us. He cares deeply about our problems.

FAST FORWARD

Join Me in My Storm!

Distribute copies of **Join Me in My Storm!** (page 94) or ask students to turn their sheets over if you made back-to-back copies. Explain this will be a very personal exercise and you will not require them to share their responses if they don't want to.

Ask your students to write a prayer to Jesus, the Weather Man. In the prayer they should name a problem they're currently facing. Then they should thank Jesus for being with them in this problem. Finally, they should ask for his help. Give your kids about three minutes to complete this assignment.

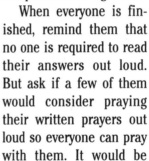

When everyone is finished, remind them that no one is required to read their answers out loud. But ask if a few of them would consider praying their written prayers out loud so everyone can pray with them. It would be great if you started the prayer time by reading a prayer of your own, addressing a problem you are currently facing. If no one else is willing to share their prayers, don't make a big deal out of it—just close your time in prayer, thanking Jesus for caring so much about our problems.

I Have a Problem with This!

Wave hello to everyone! (Oooh, you lucked out and got an easy one!)	Impersonate a chicken—actions and sounds.	Sing the national anthem.	Give a two-minute impromptu speech on how fantastic your junior high leader is.
Disco dance for 30 seconds.	Do one jumping jack. (Could it be any simpler?)	Impersonate your youth group leader (or whoever is teaching this lesson).	Blow a kiss to three people.
Imitate a cheerleader by shouting, "I've got spirit! Yes I do! I've got spirit! How 'bout you?"	Howl at the moon like a wolf.	Do one push-up.	Run around the room flapping your arms up and down while shouting, "I'm crazy as a loon! I'm crazy as a loon!"
Break dance!	Say, "I accept this dare."	Pretend you're a salmon swimming upstream.	Shout, "The Martians are coming to get me! The Martians are coming to get me!" And then run screaming out of the room. Come back.
Quote a Bible verse.	Be Richard Simmons and lead an aerobic workout for one minute (even if no one follows your lead).	Give your youth group leader a big ol' hug!	With your hands up like paws, go up to someone, bark, shake your tush like it was a tail, then lick his or her face.

THE WEATHER MAN

Read the story of the Weather Man in Mark 4:35-41 to find the answers to these questions.

1. The Weather Man's real name is—
   - ❏ Dan Frosty, the channel 7 weather reporter
   - ❏ Jesus
   - ❏ Bob
   - ❏ Mark, the author of the gospel

2. The Weather Man and _____ went out in a boat.
   - ❏ Dan Frosty, the channel 7 weather reporter
   - ❏ Bob
   - ❏ The disciples
   - ❏ Lazarus

3. What happened to them while they were out in the boat?
   - ❏ They were swallowed by a big fish, where they stayed for three days.
   - ❏ They did some serious fishin'!
   - ❏ They all got seasick and started blowin' chunks.
   - ❏ A big storm started and the waves got huge.

4. The disciples, many of whom were fishermen, knew that this kind of storm meant—
   - ❏ They were all going to get seasick and start blowin' chunks.
   - ❏ They might die.
   - ❏ Their mothers would probably say, "I told you to be careful on that boat!"
   - ❏ They would have to chill for awhile until the storm blew past.

5. During the storm, the Weather Man was—
   - ❏ Blowin' chunks.
   - ❏ Yelling, "We're all going to die!"
   - ❏ Praying.
   - ❏ Sleeping in the back of the boat.

6. After they woke him up and begged him to help, the Weather Man spoke to the storm and said—
   - ❏ "Hi there. How ya doin'?"
   - ❏ "Be still."
   - ❏ "Where's Dan Frosty, the channel 7 weather reporter?"
   - ❏ "Rock us around for an hour or so more, then get out of here."

Bonus super-duper obvious question:
7. Where was Jesus during the disciples' problem?
   - ❏ He was with them.
   - ❏ Uh...I don't know.

Join Me in My Storm!

Write a prayer to Jesus. Tell him a problem you're currently facing. Thank him for being with you in the middle of your problem. Then ask him for help with your problem.

Dear Weather Man,

Amen!

At **10 TO 20**, we create media for **ONE PURPOSE**:
TO BROADCAST LIFE'S MOST IMPORTANT MESSAGE INTO THE HEADS AND HEARTS OF TEENAGERS.

production for promotion, broadcast, conferences and curriculum

graphics, sound, animation, and digital video for CD, DVD, and event presentations

teen books, training materials, and the Wild Truth line for junior high students and leaders

event consultation, programming, production, and media presentation

If you're in youth ministry, we can help you broadcast the Message to your students.
CHECK OUT OUR MINISTRY TOOLS AT WWW.10TO20.COM

P.O. Box 604 - Del Mar, CA 92014 - 858-793-8275 - info@10to20.com

Resources from Youth Specialties

Youth Ministry Programming

Camps, Retreats, Missions, & Service Ideas (Ideas Library)
Compassionate Kids: Practical Ways to Involve Your Students in Mission and Service
Creative Bible Lessons from the Old Testament
Creative Bible Lessons in 1 & 2 Corinthians
Creative Bible Lessons in John: Encounters with Jesus
Creative Bible Lessons in Romans: Faith on Fire!
Creative Bible Lessons on the Life of Christ
Creative Bible Lessons in Psalms
Creative Junior High Programs from A to Z, Vol. 1 (A-M)
Creative Junior High Programs from A to Z, Vol. 2 (N-Z)
Creative Meetings, Bible Lessons, & Worship Ideas (Ideas Library)
Crowd Breakers & Mixers (Ideas Library)
Downloading the Bible Leader's Guide
Drama, Skits, & Sketches (Ideas Library)
Drama, Skits, & Sketches 2 (Ideas Library)
Dramatic Pauses
Everyday Object Lessons
Games (Ideas Library)
Games 2 (Ideas Library)
Good Sex: A Whole-Person Approach to Teenage Sexuality and God
Great Fundraising Ideas for Youth Groups
More Great Fundraising Ideas for Youth Groups
Great Retreats for Youth Groups
Holiday Ideas (Ideas Library)
Hot Illustrations for Youth Talks
More Hot Illustrations for Youth Talks
Still More Hot Illustrations for Youth Talks
Ideas Library on CD-ROM
Incredible Questionnaires for Youth Ministry
Junior High Game Nights
More Junior High Game Nights
Kickstarters: 101 Ingenious Intros to Just about Any Bible Lesson
Live the Life! Student Evangelism Training Kit
Memory Makers
The Next Level Leader's Guide
Play It! Over 150 Great Games for Youth Groups
Roaring Lambs
Special Events (Ideas Library)
Spontaneous Melodramas
Student Leadership Training Manual
Student Underground: An Event Curriculum on the Persecuted Church
Super Sketches for Youth Ministry
Talking the Walk
Teaching the Bible Creatively
Videos That Teach
What Would Jesus Do? Youth Leader's Kit
Wild Truth Bible Lessons
Wild Truth Bible Lessons 2
Wild Truth Bible Lessons—Pictures of God
Worship Services for Youth Groups

Professional Resources

Administration, Publicity, & Fundraising (Ideas Library)
Equipped to Serve: Volunteer Youth Worker Training Course
Help! I'm a Junior High Youth Worker!
Help! I'm a Small-Group Leader!
Help! I'm a Sunday School Teacher!
Help! I'm a Volunteer Youth Worker!
How to Expand Your Youth Ministry
How to Speak to Youth...and Keep Them Awake at the Same Time
Junior High Ministry (Updated & Expanded)
The Ministry of Nurture: A Youth Worker's Guide to Discipling Teenagers
Purpose-Driven Youth Ministry
Purpose-Driven Youth Ministry Training Kit
So That's Why I Keep Doing This! 52 Devotional Stories for Youth Workers
A Youth Ministry Crash Course
The Youth Worker's Handbook to Family Ministry

Discussion Starters

Discussion & Lesson Starters (Ideas Library)
Discussion & Lesson Starters 2 (Ideas Library)
EdgeTV
Get 'Em Talking
Keep 'Em Talking!
High School TalkSheets
More High School TalkSheets
High School TalkSheets: Psalms and Proverbs
Junior High TalkSheets
More Junior High TalkSheets
Junior High TalkSheets: Psalms and Proverbs
Real Kids: Short Cuts
Real Kids: The Real Deal—on Friendship, Loneliness, Racism, & Suicide
Real Kids: The Real Deal—on Sexual Choices, Family Matters, & Loss
Real Kids: The Real Deal—on Stressing Out, Addictive Behavior, Great Comebacks, & Violence
Real Kids: Word on the Street
Have You Ever...? 450 Intriguing Questions Guaranteed to Get Teenagers Talking
Unfinished Sentences: 450 Tantalizing Statement-Starters to Get Teenagers Talking & Thinking
What If...? 450 Thought-Provoking Questions to Get Teenagers Talking, Laughing, and Thinking
Would You Rather...? 465 Provocative Questions to Get Teenagers Talking

Art Source Clip Art

Stark Raving Clip Art (print)
Youth Group Activities (print)
Clip Art Library Version 2.0 (CD-ROM)

Digital Resources

Clip Art Library Version 2.0 (CD-ROM)
Ideas Library on CD-ROM

Videos & Video Curricula

EdgeTV
Equipped to Serve: Volunteer Youth Worker Training Course
The Heart of Youth Ministry: A Morning with Mike Yaconelli
Good Sex: A Whole-Person Approach to Teenage Sexuality and God
Live the Life! Student Evangelism Training Kit
Purpose-Driven Youth Ministry Training Kit
Real Kids: Short Cuts
Real Kids: The Real Deal—on Friendship, Loneliness, Racism, & Suicide
Real Kids: The Real Deal—on Sexual Choices, Family Matters, & Loss
Real Kids: The Real Deal—on Stressing Out, Addictive Behavior, Great Comebacks, & Violence
Real Kids: Word on the Street
Student Underground: An Event Curriculum on the Persecuted Church
Understanding Your Teenager Video Curriculum

Student Resources

Downloading the Bible: A Rough Guide to the New Testament
Downloading the Bible: A Rough Guide to the Old Testament
Grow For It Journal
Grow For It Journal through the Scriptures
Spiritual Challenge Journal: The Next Level
Teen Devotional Bible
What Would Jesus Do? Spiritual Challenge Journal
What Almost Nobody Will Tell You About Sex
Wild Truth Journal for Junior Highers
Wild Truth Journal—Pictures of God